Print ISBN: 978-1-7362800-0-3 Paperback
Print ISBN: 978-1-7362899-1-0 Hardback
ISBN: 978-1-7362800-2-7 eBook

Printed in the United States of America on SFI Certified paper.

First Edition

Visit www.elizabethmarkie.com/brains-book

Ordering Information:
For details, contact elizabeth.markie@weimagine.com.

Illustrations by Annerly Dixon
Cover design, book design and images by Marti Martin (Bridge and Bloom)

Editing by Doug Childress

Proof Reading by Dr. George Stovall

All efforts have been made to assure the accuracy of the information contained in this book as of the date of publication.

BRAINS

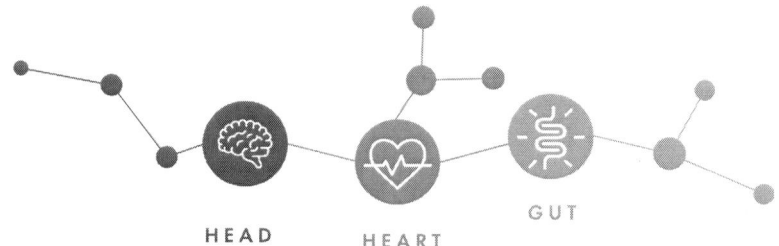

HEAD HEART GUT

TRANSFORM THE WAY YOU LIVE AND WORK.

ELIZABETH MARKIE

ART DIRECTION, DESIGN, AND FIGURES BY MARTI MARTIN

ILLUSTRATIONS BY ANNERLY DIXON

For you.

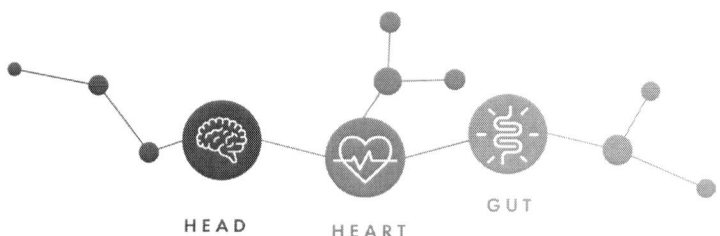

HEAD   HEART   GUT

Acknowledgments

I am full of gratitude for the gifts of my husband, Will, and son, Michael, and their vast amount of never-ending love, support, and patience.

I have a heartfelt appreciation for Andy Sriubas. He recognized the potential of Tri Brain®, created a paradigm shift in my thinking, and encouraged me to write a book.

I will forever be thankful for the perspective and support of Marti Martin and her magic.

I am grateful to Doug Childress for his guidance and patience.

And forever appreciative of the never-ending synchronicities in my life.

About the Author

Photo by Elise Elsberry

Elizabeth Markie, Founder of Welmagine, Inc.© and architect of Tri Brain®, Tri Brain® Wellness and Tri Brain Yoga® is inspired by family and deeply committed to supporting others to live fully.

She and her husband live in St. Petersburg, FL with their son and two dogs, Yeti and Mouse.

To engage in conversation with Elizabeth or learn more about her classes, workshops, speaking engagements and one-on-one support, visit ElizabethMarkie.com

ABOUT THE DESIGNER

Marti Martin is a beyond brilliant creative and magician, as well as co-founder of Bridge and Bloom.

ABOUT THE ILLUSTRATOR

Annerly Dixon is a talented Studio Art Major at Florida State University.

Table of Contents

Forward

Be the transformative change.

"When you change the way you look at things, the things you look at change."

Our world is ripe for change, and our planet has the potential to be more loving and peaceful if we choose to evolve and better understand ourselves and others. We have the power to transform our world by shifting our consciousness, transforming ourselves, and opening our hearts. Tri Brain® theory is a means by which we can accomplish this, and with the insights provided in this book, my hope is that you too will choose to be part of this rewarding experience.

With love,
Elizabeth

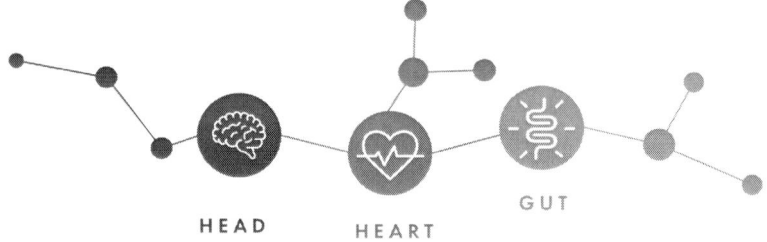

HEAD   HEART   GUT

Tri Brain®

My Why

My husband and I traded in our VW Jetta for a Subaru. The compelling feature that closed the deal was the fact that the car didn't require a key in the ignition for it to operate. I had been spending countless moments searching for my car keys, sunglasses, prescription glasses, my phone, and several other items. The fact that I could now keep my car key in my purse without having to look for it was a gift and well worth the price of the car!

Leading up to that purchase decision, my 94-year-old mother had fallen, broken her hip, and shattered her femur. Having lived independently until that moment, she required our assistance and support in recovering from her surgery and in relocating her to an assisted living facility. For those of you that have had this fairly common experience with aging parents, you understand the complexity of the many decisions and emotions that are involved. In addition to dealing with that challenge, our teenage son was in his freshman year of high school, and we had just made the decision to completely remodel our home, which required all of us to move into temporary housing. And then a few weeks later my husband was diagnosed with cancer.

When I found myself forgetting to prepare for client meetings and missing appointments, I knew the Subaru alone wasn't going to solve my problems with misplaced items. This was even more evident when I realized I couldn't stay focused long enough to learn all the fancy new technology that Subaru offered. Despite practicing yoga daily, being a certified HeartMath Resilience trainer, and being deeply immersed in the study and teaching the neuroscience of our three brains, I wasn't immune to my own brains' reaction to threat and my body's natural stress response. The challenges that life had brought to me all at once was more than I was prepared to handle at that moment in time.

Life brings us many experiences and provides us the opportunity to learn some very valuable lessons. Some are perceived as wonderful and inherently fulfilling, and some are viewed as tremendous challenges and hardships. They can present themselves in the form of relationships, sudden events, and other life-changing experiences. But in each instance, how we choose to react to these experiences, and our ability to learn from them, depends largely upon our mindset. Recognizing this simple fact can go a long way in helping us adapt and overcome major challenges in our lives.

In retrospect, I can't imagine how I might have reacted to the array of life circumstances that presented themselves to me without having the knowledge that I am sharing with you in this book. It has allowed me to become an observer as well as an active participant in my life, and as a result, I was able to avoid going through life on autopilot. With the tools I have since learned, and that I will happily share with you, I have learned to respond in a more proactive and constructive way to my environment rather than reacting to it emotionally. And while I am far from perfect in doing this consistently, the improvements that I have made have made a tremendous impact on the quality of my life, especially during the Covid-19 pandemic. These are the gifts that I would like to share with you so that you can better handle life's ups and downs and realize your life's greatest potential in the process.

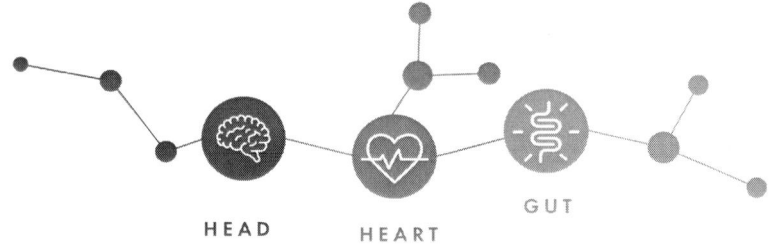

HEAD   HEART   GUT

Introduction

Knowledge is power: Get to know your three brains

The brain in your head is not the only brain in your body. In fact, you might be surprised to know that you have three brains. In addition to the brain situated within your skull, your heart and your gut are also brains that influence how you respond to life experiences. At first, this may sound a bit unrealistic. After all, the heart and gut are not capable of planning, imagining, or creating like our cognitive brain. But our hearts and gut do have extensive neurological systems that are capable of learning and retaining memory. Because of this, they can well be considered additional "brains" that exist within our bodies. And recognizing this fact is quite important in our efforts to achieve better holistic wellness.

There is plenty of information available about how to keep your brain, heart, and gut healthy. This book is not about that. Its purpose is to provide you with an understanding of how and why your three brains function and how they interact in a way to optimize your wellbeing. Our world has become full of "specialists" who are knowledgeable about specific organ systems and parts of the body. We have brain specialists, gut specialists, as well as heart specialists. But while this has provided many insights about each special area, this approach has failed to address how these systems of intelligence rely on the function and health of the others. In other words, holistic wellness has been neglected because we have focused too much on the trees without considering the forest.

When your three brains are well integrated and effectively aligned, your capacity to function at your very best is significantly enhanced. This alignment and integration enable you to completely transform your approach to life, and in the process, you gain an ability to pursue wellness at a much higher level. While many resources are available that can teach us about each brain, it's important to appreciate that they do not operate independently. Your three brains actually "talk" to one another. The brain, heart, and gut nervous systems combine in ways that creates your behavior, and many times, you are completely unaware of these interactions. But when you learn how each of these brains communicate and interact with one another, you can start to make a conscious connection and enhance this entire communication process.

Knowledge is power. When you understand the neuroscience behind how your head, heart, and gut brains interact, you improve your ability to better manage your thinking, achieve emotional agility, and reduce your body's stress response. As a result, you become better able to achieve holistic health and wellbeing. And at the same time, you will also gain the capacity to enhance your relationships as you expand your understanding of yourself and others. For many individuals, this level of knowledge and understanding is nonexistent, and an awareness of how the three brains interact is lacking. But once this knowledge is acquired, you will gain a conscious awareness of these interactions that can be used to better guide your responses. With this in mind, this book seeks to offer this knowledge so that you can use that information to better manage all aspects of your life.

The knowledge I have acquired in the field of neuroscience has been relatively recent. Earlier in my life, I held various leadership positions in hospitality, sales, operations, market research, and brand marketing. Interestingly, my leadership style was not something learned from a textbook or even from leadership courses. Instead, my leadership approach developed more organically. I always had a natural talent to think strategically and see connections among various issues and concepts. This ability to perceive correlations and interrelationships served me well in business when developing strategic initiatives and developing processes and procedures. But at the same time, I also relied just as much on intuition and gut instincts and what emotionally felt like the right thing to do. This approach to decision-making has been true in all aspects of my life, not just in business.

After leaving the corporate world, I embarked on a new career journey as a personal and professional development coach.

My initial interest in neuroscience began when I was looking to better define my approach to personal and professional development coaching overall. I've always been curious about how our brains work. So, when I learned there was a coaching certification program designed around the most recent neuroscientific discoveries involving the brain, I enrolled. After completing the NeuroLeadership Institute's brain-based coaching certification program, I was completely hooked and hungry for more. As a result, I then enrolled in the Foundations of NeuroLeadership and subsequently participated in Dr. Sarah McKay's Neuroscience Academy's training certification in brain health. Thus, while I am not a formally trained as a neuroscientist, I have certainly gained a tremendous amount of knowledge of the field.

As I learned more about the field of neuroscience, I became interested in neurobiology and began to explore other areas of neuroscience beyond the brain. In the process, I discovered that the heart and the gut are also classified as brains. Because the heart and gut also have nervous systems as well as the ability to learn and retain information, they can be classified as a brain as well. With this insight, I then discovered the HeartMath Institute where I learned more about the science of the heart. The education received from the HeartMath Institute provided a strong foundation of knowledge related to the heart's nervous system and how it interacts with the cognitive brain. And eventually, this led to my certification as a HeartMath Resilience Trainer. It was becoming increasingly clear that neuroscience involved much more than cognitive neuroscience alone.

With a strong foundation of knowledge in neuroscience in cognitive and heart areas, I then explored the neuroscience of the gut. When it comes to this area of neuroscience, what we know about the gut brain, at this time, is still quite limited. But the latest research and information has revealed some exciting findings. In addition to interactions between the gut's nervous system and both the heart and cognitive brains, new insights about our body's microbiome and its interactions with the nervous system are also evident. With a desire to learn more about the gut brain, and with a passion for self-discovery, I have read extensively on the subject. And while this field specifically remains in its infancy, a significant amount of research already supports the importance of the gut brain on holistic health and wellness. The more I have learned, the more passionate I have become about understanding neuroscience at a deeper level. And this is what has led to the insights that I have since gained concerning the importance of our tri-brains and their role in promoting total wellness.

I am deeply committed to sharing with you what I've learned about the neuroscience of our three brains. I have experienced and witnessed how this information helps to facilitate positive outcomes in people's lives, including my own. My intention is not to tell you how to change, what to eat, or how much to exercise in order to ensure the health of your brains. Instead, I simply wish to provide you with an understanding of how your head, heart, and gut brains function and interact in a practical way so that you can discover new insights about yourself and others. This knowledge alone is enough to help you choose a better way to approach life that leads to you to greater happiness, fulfillment, and wellbeing.

This book is not meant to be a quick read, although you may choose to use it in this way. However, I encourage you to stop and think about the concepts in this book as you proceed section to section. Reflect how the information applies to you on a moment-to-moment basis. Relate these insights to your experiences and perceptions, to your inherent beliefs, and to your actions and behaviors throughout each day. In doing so, you will likely find that you are no longer operating on "auto-pilot" but instead responding to your environment in a constructive and thoughtful way rather than simply reacting to it. This is the potential that an understanding of Tri Brain$^{®}$ can offer, and I look forward to sharing these insights with you in an effort to enhance your quality of life now and in the future.

The Head Brain

An understanding of how your brain functions allows you to better manage your thinking, emotions, and behavior.

Know Thy Brain, Know Thyself

Understand the basic principles of how your brain functions to better manage your thinking, emotions, and behavior

In the not so distant past, our knowledge of the brain was quite limited. Its anatomy was revealed through dissections with advancing techniques to see the brain's structure under the microscope. Likewise, we were able to grasp some understanding of how different brain regions functioned based on the deficits that result after injury or damage. However, remarkable technologies today have greatly expanded our understanding of the brain. Magnetic resonance imaging (MRI), functional MRI, electrical neuro-technologies, and advanced brain scanning techniques have provided us new insights. These insights have certainly expanded our knowledge about the brain's anatomy and structure, and they have similarly shown us much about how our brain reacts to our experiences, our thoughts, and our emotions. And these new discoveries are having profound impacts on almost every aspect of our lives.

With a greater appreciation of our brain's inner workings, numerous disciplines have completely changed their approaches. Naturally, these discoveries have made an impact on healthcare practices, but other areas are also using these new insights to change their practices as well. Certainly, we are changing educational strategies to enhance learning, but likewise, these discoveries are also changing how militaries operate and train. And the impacts that new brain insights have made on the business world are nothing short of revolutionary. Specifically, our knowledge of the brain is responsible for neuro-linguistic programming (NLP), which is an integral part of business leadership development, marketing, communications, and training.

Despite these advances, neuroscience remains in an infancy stage of development and understanding. The complex nature of our brains suggest that many more discoveries are yet to be made. Fortunately, however, understanding all the known complexities of the brain to date isn't required for you to evoke positive changes in your thinking and actions. For this reason, I will not be addressing the brain's intricate structures or its complex functions in detail. Instead, "brain basics" will be discussed only to the extent needed for you to take conscious control over your thoughts and behaviors. With this basic level of understanding, you will be able to consciously manage your brain and pursue those goals you wish to achieve.

YOUR BRAIN: THE ORIGINAL SUPERCOMPUTER

Believe it or not, but your brain has approximately 84 billion nerve cells (neurons)! Even more amazing is the fact that these billions of neurons have over 100 trillion connections with one another that are actively being used every second. Each neuron has the potential to receive and send electrical signals traveling around 250 mph, which creates an incredible network of brain activity. This network enables us to think, feel, and store memories while also regulating thousands if not millions of bodily functions. When I think of this constant brain activity that is actively ongoing, I imagine having an electrical storm inside my head! Without question, the brain is an incredibly complex machine that performs an astounding number of tasks each and every moment.

As you readily recognize, your brain has the ability to think, process, and form memories. But one of the fascinating aspects of the brain is its ability to store prior information and memories for easy retrieval later. In essence, your brain "hardwires" these memories so that you can readily access them at a later time. In addition, your brain also has the ability to become more adept at routine tasks the more they are practiced. In both cases, new pathways and connections are formed, which is the foundation of neuroplasticity. But in order to better understand how this evolves, it first requires a basic appreciation of how neurons communicate and function with one another.

Neurons communicate with one another through a connection known as a synapse. This point of contact where the projection of one neuron meets another utilizes both electrical and chemical signals to communicate information. The neuron sending information does so by sending an electrical signal down its projection (called an axon) until it reaches the synapse. At that point, the electrical signal triggers the release of a neurochemical (called a neurotransmitter) into the synapse space, which travels across the tiny cleft to the other neuron's projection (called a dendrite). Once this neurotransmitter reaches that side, it then triggers another electrical signal that takes the information to that neuron.

This series of events can take place repeatedly and involve thousands of neurons in the process.

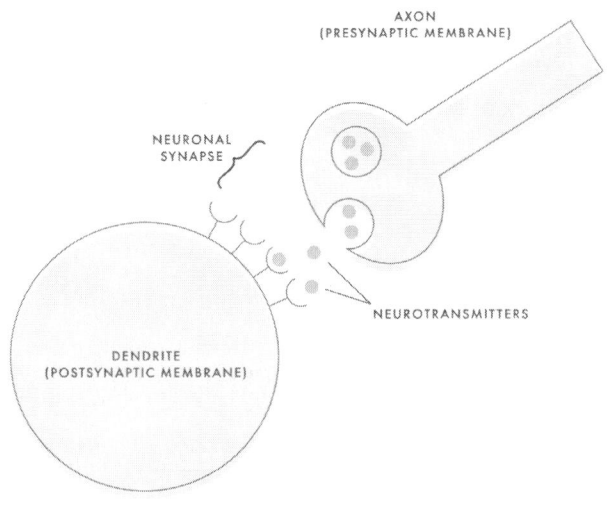

FIGURE 1 - NEURONAL SYNAPSE[1]

Most of you likely recognize the term neurotransmitters, also referred to as neurochemicals, and in all likelihood, probably know a few of the more common ones. For example, you may recognize the neurotransmitter dopamine, which has been labelled the "feel good" chemical encouraging us to pursue activities that are pleasing. Serotonin is another commonly referenced neurotransmitter, which has been linked to mood conditions like anxiety and depression. In actuality, however, there are several neurotransmitters that have been discovered to date, and each of these serve as important chemical messengers between neurons. Depending on the neurotransmitter and its effects on a neuron, different physical and psychological effects can result. This might involve your heart rate, your appetite, and even your mood change. And they also influence our attention, memory, and emotions.

It should also be pointed out that the influences that neurochemicals have do not represent a one-way street. In fact, you have the ability to potentially change the chemical make-up and distribution of these chemicals in your brain based on your thoughts and behaviors. By changing your pattern of thinking or performing specific activities, neurochemical profiles can also change. Or to put it another way, your body will be better able to recognize your mindset. For example, when you think of someone or something for which you are grateful, neurotransmitters like dopamine and norepinephrine are generated, and you will experience a general sense of joy.

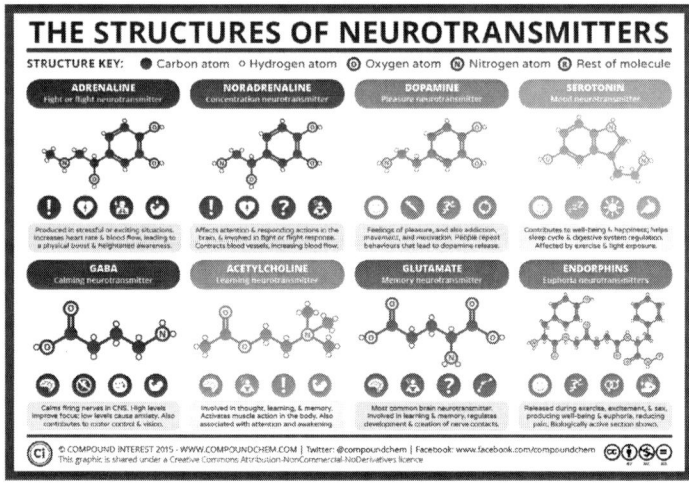

FIGURE 2 - NEUROTRANSMITTERS IN THE BRAIN[2]

HABITS AND PERCEPTIONS ARE HARDWIRED IN NEUROPATHWAYS

In considering brain connections among neurons, the more a series of connections are used, the more entrenched they become. Therefore, over time, frequently used connections establish neuropathways that become much easier and faster for electrical and chemical signals to travel. This is essential so that we can make greater sense of the world around us and function more effectively. For example, wouldn't it be frustrating if every time you sat down in the driver's seat of car you had to learn all over again how to drive? Absolutely! But because our brains are able to create neuropathways among commonly traveled neuron connections, such frustrations can be avoided. Let's think about this another way. Have you ever encountered a tall field of grass while walking outdoors? If you were the first person to walk the field, then you likely struggled to find your way. But if several others had already traveled across the field, there was probably a path for you to follow. The same analogy can be made when pouring a cup of water on a pile of sand. The first pour will create channels in the sand along which the water will travel. And when subsequent cups of water are poured on the pile, the water tends to follow the same channels already formed. In essence, this is the same phenomenon that occurs in the brain when it forms neuropathways.

Neuroscientists have a saying that, "cells that fire together, wire together." In other words, the more frequently neurons connect and communicate with one another, the more likely they are to establish a neuropathway. This is often called "hardwiring," since these established neuropathways are also what allows us to store information, knowledge, and memories. At the same time, hardwiring is what causes us to continually think, feel, and react the same way over and over again. In essence, the hardwiring effects that neuropathways create not only facilitate our ability to retain information, but they also contribute to habitual thoughts, emotions, and behaviors.

One of the biggest challenges in creating new neuropathways stems from the fact that we are not consciously aware that our current thoughts, feelings, and behaviors are already hardwired in our brains. According to Dr. Joe Dispenza, author of Breaking the Habit of Being Yourself, roughly 95 percent of who you are by age 35 years can be attributed to established neuropathways. Our emotional reactions, beliefs, perceptions, and attitudes as well as our internal thoughts mainly reflect well-established patterns of brain activity and function. But all of this happens in an unconscious manner without most of us being aware that this is occurring. And this helps explain why it is often difficult to break habits and adopt new ones.[3]

Certainly, some brain functions share similar neuropathways among individuals. For example, the brain's ability to voluntarily move your right hand will use a very similar neuropathway for most people. But the same is not true for more complex brain functions. Your beliefs, thoughts, and perceptions will be notably different from someone else's because your life experiences have not been the same. The social encounters you have had, the challenges in life you have faced, and your successes and failures are unique to you. Therefore, the neuropathways that have been hardwired in your brain will naturally be different from another person's. The bottom line is that no two people are hardwired the same, and as a result, no two people will have the same perceptions either.

YOUR BRAIN IS TRYING TO KEEP YOU ALIVE

When it comes to your brain, it has one essential and fundamental operating principle… to keep you alive! Given that many threats exist in life, and some environments are quite risky to our health, our brain's primary task is to constantly scan our surroundings to determine how best to respond. In some instances, our brain identifies the essential things we need, such as food, water, and positive experiences. In other circumstances, our brain recognizes potential harms or threats and steers us in the opposite direction. In both cases, our brain is simply trying to protect us while making sure we attain the things we need to stay healthy and alive. This "threat versus reward" assessment is inherent to our brain's nature.

As you might imagine, this instinct to constantly assess threat and reward in the environment has been present for millions of years. Of course, in the past, threats in the environment were much more serious, such as whether or not a lion, tiger, or bear was about to have us for lunch. Or whether or not someone might be trying to harm us or help us. While these types of threats are not common today for the majority of human beings, our brain continues to operate on this same fundamental principle of survival. The only difference is that today's threats are not quite as obvious. Rather than feeling threatened by wild animals we now feel threatened by traffic jams, unanswered emails, and daily financial pressures. In fact, our very own thoughts and worries about tomorrow may trigger these same brain reactions today.

The key point related to this unique feature of our brains relates to the influence our thoughts have over our reactions and behaviors. In situations where threat is perceived, regardless whether it's a lion or overdue mortgage payment, our brain triggers emotions based on these perceptions and predications that provoke a response. The same thing occurs when something is perceived as beneficial and rewarding. Therefore, how we perceive various aspects of our life and our environment affects how we think, feel, and act. If we can simply appreciate these perceptions at a conscious level, then we gain the ability to alter these reactions at a root level. While perceiving threats and rewards are inherently important for survival, it doesn't always mean our brains get it right. For this reason, being more conscious and aware of these perceptions is important to better ensure our responses are appropriate.

ORGANIZING PRINCIPLE

AWAY FROM
THREAT

TOWARD
REWARD

CHANGE YOUR THOUGHTS, SHIFT YOUR FEELINGS AND BEHAVIORS

Having discussed how our brains become hardwired over time through repetitive thoughts that stimulate the same neural pathways, it is now important to talk about how this affects our behaviors and achievements. In this regard, the Iceberg Model provides a nice schematic to highlight how this process works. The Iceberg Model portrays a concept related to systems thinking that connects brain function to actual behaviors.

And in the process, it explains how thoughts and feelings are responsible for driving our actions as well as our achievements in life.

In the Iceberg Model, a smaller portion exists above the water line while a larger part is hidden from view beneath the water. In terms of this water line, consider this the border between what we consciously see and observe and what is often subconscious in nature. As a result, our actual behaviors, actions, and habits that we routinely perform are conscious in nature. In other words, we (as well as others) can observe our actions and appreciate what we are able to achieve. But at a level that is not often considered consciously, we have thoughts and emotions that drive these actions. And it is these thoughts and feelings that are important to recognize and appreciate.

ICEBERG MODEL

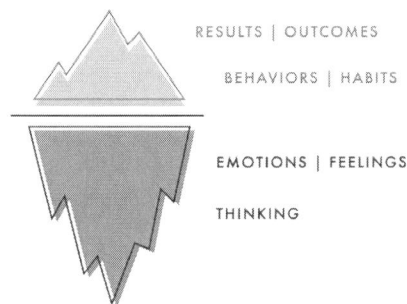

RESULTS | OUTCOMES

BEHAVIORS | HABITS

EMOTIONS | FEELINGS

THINKING

What we achieve is driven by how we think and feel.

As evident in the Iceberg Model diagram, the base foundation of the iceberg is grounded upon the thoughts we have on a regular basis. Similarly, the emotions and feelings we have in relation to our thoughts serve as support for our behaviors and actions as well. With this in mind, consider you set a goal to exercise every morning. This goal, which would be an observable, conscious action, would be more likely to occur if you thought exercise was important to your wellbeing, and if you were emotionally motivated to exercise. In contrast, if your beliefs and feelings were more ambivalent in nature, your ability to achieve your exercise goal would be much less likely.

When I first came across the Iceberg Model and its explanation for behaviors, I was initially under the impression that my emotions were the primary driver of my reactions and behaviors. But at the heart of these feelings are thoughts, which can be influenced consciously. These electrical connections within our brain creates a chemical reaction that triggers emotions and how we feel. And subsequently, these feelings affect what we think about thereafter. A "thinking-feeling-thinking" loop develops that can be difficult to interrupt. But fortunately, we can choose to change these thoughts, which then changes how we feel and behave.

Consider the following example. Suppose you awake and begin thinking about a challenging project at work that day, the traffic you will face during your morning commute, and that long list of unopened emails. These thoughts naturally trigger feelings of dread, which may then evolve into resentment or even anger. In turn, you may then take out these feelings on others around you by being short-tempered. Alternatively, if you choose to think positive thoughts upon awakening about your day, you will be more likely to feel grateful and optimistic. This then encourages more pleasant interactions with others as a result.

In bringing this back to our neural pathways' discussion, it is important to recognize that thinking the same thoughts and holding onto the same beliefs can prevent us from pursuing new achievements and goals. If we want to change our habits, behaviors and actions, then we must start at the very foundation. By making an effort to change the way we perceive, think, and feel about things, we invite new opportunities of achievement into our lives. But until we delve into those less conscious thoughts and emotions, our ability to realize these positive changes will be quite limited. Fortunately, existing neural pathways that generate these thoughts and feelings can be altered. And in the process, we can enhance our ability to attain a variety of life goals we may have thought were impossible to achieve.

CHANGE YOUR BRAIN

One of the most compelling reasons for you to know how your brain works is because you can actively influence your brain's ability to function. For example, you can solve a problem by thinking about the issue and exploring your memories, knowledge, and other insights. At the same time, you also appreciate the fact that you can enhance your brain's abilities by attending school and gaining education that improves your intellect. You may likewise repeatedly practice an activity, like playing an instrument, that facilitates your proficiency and skills. And certainly, brain rehabilitation after illness or injury is well recognized as a way to change how your brain functions. These types of personal observations are enough to convince you that you have the capacity to change your brain, at least to some extent.

Despite this, it was previously believed that the brain had essentially reached a permanent level of development by the time a person reached the age of twenty-five years. While small changes in the brain might be seen after that age, these weren't believed to be very substantial. However, new technological insights and a deeper understanding of the brain have encouraged us to revisit this belief and its accuracy. It is now apparent that the brain has a tremendous capacity to change, even later in life. Over the course of the last century and a half, we have come to appreciate that the brain is actually a very adaptive organ throughout the lifespan. And we have labelled this intriguing aspect of the brain as neuroplasticity.

Neuroplasticity describes the brain's ability to form and reorganize throughout life in response to learning or experience. This phenomenon is most noticeable after injury to the brain, but it is also at work even in the absence of injury. The idea that the brain was not permanently fixed throughout adulthood was originally proposed in 1890 by an American psychologist and philosopher, William James. Likewise, around this same time, the work of Spanish neuroanatomist Santiago Ramon y Cajal was also supportive of this concept. Cajal offered his cerebral gymnastics hypothesis that suggested the brain had the ability to change its number of connections between neurons. And in 1893, Italian neuropsychiatrist Eugenio Tanzi postulated that enhanced neuron function and connections could be fostered through specific learning and repeated practice. All of these discoveries and theories described what we now call neuroplasticity.

Despite these theories, people remained stuck in their belief that "you can't teach an old dog new tricks" for many decades to follow. These persistent beliefs hindered progress in several ways. For some, this belief provided an excuse for resisting change because they attributed their faults to the way their brain was "hardwired." Likewise, these notions undermined progress in other areas like healthcare. Care for stroke patients or brain injured individuals took a "wait and see" approach rather than pursuing more proactive measures of care. Fortunately, that is no longer where we stand today as more recent revelations in science has completely shifted our thinking as well as our actions.

Over the course of the last decade, several scientific discoveries have fueled the idea that our brains have a tremendous capacity to change well into adulthood. Some researchers have separated these concepts into two types of neuroplasticity, functional and structural. Functional neuroplasticity refers to the capacity of our brain to adapt when new functional demands are required. A perfect example of this would be a stroke patient where unaffected areas of the brain compensate for the parts of the brain damaged by the stroke. Function is regained as these other brain areas adapt.

Structural neuroplasticity, on the other hand, refers to actual changes in the brain's neuron connections. For example, repeated practice and targeted learning (known as cognitive training) have been shown to increase the number of neuron connections known as synapses in relevant brain regions. And even newer techniques like deep brain stimulation, visual feedback, and medications are being explored today for their capacity to promote neuroplasticity change.[5]

As individuals develop greater self-awareness and evoke positive changes in their lives, they experience changes in their thinking and knowledge that support what science is discovering about the brain's neuroplasticity potential. Several documented stories now highlight this tremendous potential for our brains to change well into old age. Specifically, Dr. Norman Doidge's book, The Brain That Changes Itself: Stories of Personal Triumph from the Frontiers of Brain Science, chronicles the events of several individuals who experience seemingly miraculous changes resulting from neuroplasticity effects. In the book, individuals with congenital brain defects, stroke, mental health conditions, and intellectual challenges were all able to enjoy remarkable improvements through tools and techniques that stimulated neuroplasticity change.[6]

Some aspects of neuroplasticity can be explained through the effects that neurochemicals evoke in the brain over time. Since these chemicals can mediate changes in the brain's structure and function that result from specific learning or repeated actions, they also play a role in neuroplasticity. Thus, you can appreciate how understanding how synapses and neurotransmitters work can greatly assist you in choosing strategies that allow you to change in a desired direction. In other words, if we really wish to change our habits, we must harness the power of neuroplasticity and create new neuropathways to replace old ones.

From my own personal experience, I have been fortunate enough to witness neuroplasticity in action during my work in self-growth and personal development. I am consistently amazed at the ability for individuals to evolve and overcome challenges. And by invoking the brain's neuroplasticity potential, such positive changes can be realized within a short period of time. But in order to truly tap into your brain's incredible capacity for adapting, two things are required. One is a strong motivation to change, and the other is a good understanding of how your brain operates and functions. With these in place, your potential to achieve long-lasting and positive changes in your life are tremendous no matter what age you are.

BRAIN INFLUENCES: HOW YOUR BRAIN DEVELOPS, ADAPTS AND FUNCTIONS

THE BOTTOM UP, OUTSIDE IN, AND TOP DOWN MODEL

When it comes to your brain, it is quite amazing in its overall abilities. Your brain processes your experiences, it stores your memories, it enables you to feel emotions, and it gives you your "personality." You might be aware of these types of functions that your brain provides, but you might be less aware of the array of influences that affect these brain functions. While your brain is somewhat influenced by genetics, your brain and personality are actually affected to a greater extent by your environment and through your experiences. Even the types of thoughts and feelings you encounter affect your brain in substantial ways. In other words, **your experiences, thoughts, actions, and emotions are all constantly changing the make-up of your brain.**

In an effort to better appreciate how your brain is influenced by an array of factors, the Biopsychosocial Model of Health offers a framework. This model describes how various psychological, sociological, and biological influences affects how your brain develops, adapts, and functions. Dr. Sarah McKay, neuroscientist and founder of The Neuroscience Academy, utilized this as a framework to develop her own model entitled the Bottom-Up, Outside-In and Top-Down Model of Brain Health.[7] In doing so, she simplified the ability to understand how your brain's structure and function can be altered in an effort to achieve positive change.

In breaking down Dr. McKay's model further, the "Bottom-Up" component refers to various biological and physiological factors that affect your brain's wellbeing and function. For example, genetics can certainly affect your brain's structure and function, but at the same time, so can changes in hormone levels, immune system fluctuations, and various neurochemicals. While these influences originate within the body and brain, a number of behaviors and choices can alter these influences. Specifically, nutrition, exercise, and sleep can be used to promote better brain health and function. Likewise, avoidance of toxins and other unhealthy substances can similarly improve biological and physiological function that has a positive impact on your brain. Understanding this, the "Bottom-Up" component of Dr. McKay's model represents the "bio" aspect of the biopsychosocial framework.[8]

Next is the "Outside-In" portion of Dr. McKay's model. As you may have guessed, outside influences that affect your brain's health and function are those in your immediate environment. At first glance, you may assume this refers to the air we breathe and the areas we live. But outside influences are much more comprehensive than this. The interactions we have with others can have a profound effect on our brains as can the level of social support we enjoy. Likewise, the level of stress we experience on a day-to-day basis can also influence brain health in addition to other life events. The "Outside-In" aspect of the model thus correlates with the "social" component of the biopsychosocial framework.[9]

Lastly, Dr. McKay describes the "Top-Down" aspect of her model, which refers to the "psycho" portion of the biopsychosocial framework. This component describes those influences within your mind that influence your brain's wellness and function internally. For example, your mindset and your beliefs can have a significant effect on how your brain operates. Similarly, the types of thoughts that you allow as well as the emotions that you feel can similarly affect how your brain reacts.[10] Collectively, all three of these components account for the way your brain functions over time, and they also represent several areas where we can consciously influence these responses.

While Dr. McKay's model as well as the biopsychosocial framework suggest that each of these three sources of influence are separate, they actually are part of an integrated system. In other words, not only can one system affect brain health and function, but it may also interact with the other systems to impact your brain. For example, high levels of

psychological stress are known to increase blood pressure and heart disease, and both of these can then negatively affect the brain. Alternatively, relaxation techniques and exercise can lower stress, which can then improve brain function through both psychological and biological effects. And social isolation or engagement is well known to have secondary mental health and psychological effects. With this in mind, it is evident that this model embraces holistic wellness concepts that recognizes that the whole is more than simply a sum of its parts.

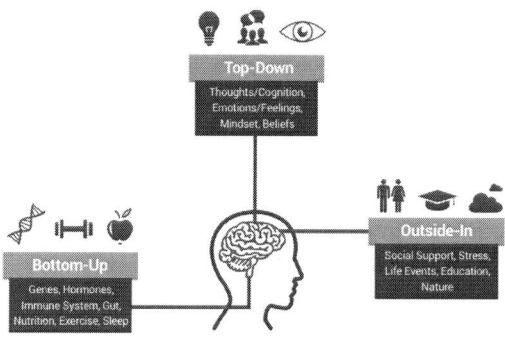

FIGURE 3- MCKAY'S BRAIN HEALTH MODEL[11]

THE COMPLEX RELATIONSHIP BETWEEN YOUR BRAIN, YOUR MIND AND YOUR CONSCIOUSNESS

Have you ever wondered how the mind differs from the brain? Likewise, have you ever considered the concept of consciousness and its actual origins? For some, the terms brain and mind are essentially the same. In other words, the mind, which defines who we are and acknowledges our vast experiences, is believed to be totally housed within the brain by some. However, increasingly, scientists from an array of fields are beginning to appreciate that the mind is much more than simply our brains. While our minds certainly involve our brains in many capacities, our minds also exist beyond our brains. In other words, the brain is simply one tool that our minds use to help perceive ourselves and our surroundings.

The reason that it is important to distinguish the mind from the brain is because the mind is believed to be the seat of our consciousness. While our brains are composed on physical structures of neurons and their connections, our minds are the conscious result of these connections and their interactions. In addition, our mind also includes interactions beyond the mind, such as those we encounter with other people, other environments, and a host of other external stimuli. From this, the mind evolves as a self-organizing system that has both internal and external features and regulates the flow of energy and information within us and among us. And it is this system of processes that define consciousness.[12]

"Brain and mind are not the same. Your brain is part of the visible, tangible world of the body. Your mind is part of the invisible transcendent world of thought, feeling, attitude, belief and imagination. The brain is the physical organ most associated with mind and consciousness, but the mind is not confined to the brain. The intelligence of your mind permeates every cell of your body, not just brain cells." - **William B. Salt II, M.D.**[13]

Certainly, this is a challenging concept to grasp, but one analogy helps place the complex relationship between brain, mind, and consciousness in perspective. Dan Siegel, a professor of psychiatry at UCLA School of Medicine, and author of the book, Mind: A Journey to the Heart of Being Human[14], describes being asked to define a shoreline. In his effort to do so, he realized he could not simply define a shoreline by describing the coast alone.

He also needed to consider the ocean or sea in this perspective. Similarly, the mind cannot be adequately defined by simply describing the brain. Its full definition requires consideration of interactions and experiences we have outside of our bodies beyond the brain. Consciousness is simply the self-organizing byproduct of the mind's internal and external complex features. To fully appreciate a shoreline, multiple perspectives must be considered. And to fully appreciate the mind, we must also look beyond the brain and consider a broader perspective in our efforts to understand consciousness.

The brain is the most complex part of the human body, it is a network of electrical and chemical activity and its vast complexity leaves much more to be revealed. In the following sections, I address only three areas of the brain: The Prefrontal Cortex, referred to as the "executive center;" the Limbic System, involved in processing memories, habits, and emotions; and the Substantia Nigra, known as the novelty center. By understanding some of the key functions of these brain centers you will be able to better manage your thinking, emotions, and behavior.

BRAIN BASICS SUMMARY POINTS

- The brain is the most complex and intriguing organs within the human body

- Our brains have a tremendous capacity to store memories and information while allowing us to feel emotions and portray a personality

- New technologies are rapidly revealing incredible new insights about the brain's structure and function

- Biopsychosocial models provide the best frameworks for understanding brain function with the Bottom up – Outside in – Top down model highlighting how the brain is integrated

- The brain is an intricate and integrated system of trillions of electrical and chemical connections among nerve cells (neurons)

- Connections between neurons are called synapses where electrical signals stimulate the release of neurotransmitters in an effort to provide inter-neuronal communications

- Neural pathways are formed along a series of neuron connections, and these can become "hardwired" with repeated use

- When we think the same thoughts repeatedly, these patterns become hardwired into our brains

- By the time we are 35 years of age, 95 percent of our personality has been hardwired through these frequently used neural pathways

- The Iceberg Model describes how thoughts drive feelings and subsequently behaviors and achievements

- A thinking-feeling-thinking loop can develop that can be difficult to break and lead to unwanted behaviors

- Threat – reward systems guide the brains responses instinctively leading us away from threats and toward positive rewards

- Modern threats are less tangible leading to false perceptions about actual threats mentally

- We have the capacity to change our thinking and perceptions through enhanced consciousness

- Neuroplasticity, which is the brain's ability to adapt throughout the lifespan, allows the brain to reform and reorganize in response to new learning and experiences

- By changing thoughts and perceptions through enhanced consciousness, we can engage neuroplasticity mechanisms and achieve positive change

- The mind extends beyond the physical structure of the brain to include interactions with others and our environment

- Consciousness is the self-organizing process of the mind that regulates the flow of energy and information within us and among us

- Tapping into our mind's consciousness invites opportunities for constructive change in life

PREFRONTAL
CORTEX

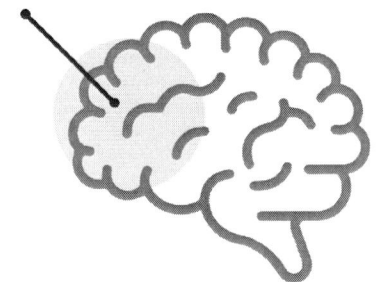

Get to Know Your Life's CEO: The Prefrontal Cortex

Your conscious brain—the prefrontal cortex—is like your life's CEO. It's running the show but it needs your support.

POWER IN PROBLEM-SOLVING

Having discussed brain basics, you have some grasp of the basic workings of the brain and how it is able to generate thoughts, feelings, and perceptions. Likewise, you have some concept of how neuroplasticity works in allowing the brain to change and adapt. With this level of understanding, there are a few other important parts of the brain that deserve more detailed attention. Because of the role these areas serve in our thinking, our emotions, and our overall awareness, each warrants a closer look so we may better understand our brain's functional capacities. The first of these areas we will consider will be the prefrontal cortex (PFC), which is often referred to as the executive center of our brain.

When you think about an executive, what comes to mind? For many of us, we think of the CEO of some major corporation who is in charge of making the big decisions, planning strategies, and making sure everything goes smoothly. In a very similar way, our PFC does the same thing in terms of brain function. In essence, our PFC is what is referred to as our **conscious brain** that allows us to better understand the world around us. It is responsible for putting together pieces of information so that the best decisions can be made and difficult problems can be solved. And it helps keep our feelings in check so we make rational decisions rather than choices triggered by emotions. In many ways, our PFC works just like a CEO.

In terms of location, the PFC portion of the brain is located in the very front part of the skull just behind the forehead. Likewise, this region is not tremendously large in size. In terms of the overall brain, it comprises only about 4 to 5 percent of the brain's total mass. Because of this, the PFC does not have a large capacity to store memory and information. Instead, the PFC tends to operate more like the working memory on your computer. While it can access broad areas of the brain including memory storage areas, it tends to store only a small amount of information while it seeks to address a specific issue or problem. The role that the PFC plays does not require holding onto information for long periods of time. Instead, it simply needs to temporarily store relevant information that allows it to complete a specific task. This is important to appreciate not only because it describes the types of function for which the PFC is responsible, but it also highlights some of the PFC's limitations.

Understanding the small size and limited capacity of the PFC to store memory and information, it's not surprising that the PFC operates best when it can focus on a select few tasks. When we are faced with multiple tasks that need to be completed at once, our PFC can become overwhelmed, which can lead to mistakes and errors. Likewise, distractions like noise, interruptions, and even our own inner dialogue can interfere with PFC function at times. When this happens, we are certainly not our best, and because of this, it is important to appreciate how we might enhance our planning, problem-solving, and executive brain functions by creating a more attractive situation.

SQUIRREL! YOUR PREFRONTAL CORTEX IS EASILY DISTRACTED

Consider the following situation. It's the middle of a workday, and you are on your way to an important business meeting while driving in the car. As you drive along, you begin to anticipate the topics that will be raised at the meeting, and you also begin to plan what you might say in response. Then, for no apparent reason, you begin to think about how you can be on time to pick up your child from school, what you will prepare for dinner that evening, and whether you might have time afterwards to pay bills. Before you know it, you have overwhelmed your PFC and no longer know the key points you wanted to make at the meeting. And in fact, you very well may make a wrong turn or fail to get off on the right exit because your PFC was so preoccupied with other tasks.

One way to envision your PFC is by thinking of it as your brain's window to the world. When awake, everything we encounter is perceived and processed by our PFC to some extent. Some of these stimuli may be quickly recognized as insignificant and discounted while others will attract greater attention. But regardless, your PFC still takes the time to examine your environment and the interactions being encountered, big and small. While this sounds quite appealing in many ways, it also means that your PFC is **prone to being distracted**, especially when you are involved in situations that are highly stimulating.

Of course, your PFC not only attends to external stimulations but to internal ones as well. The thoughts that you generate internally within your mind also get the attention of your PFC. Because these thoughts often pose issues and problems themselves, the PFC feels the need to address these thoughts as well. Therefore, the more concerns we have, the more likely our PFC will become distracted as well. Even if we are sitting at quiet desk without any external distractions at all, our thoughts can still cause our PFC to function less well if they are constantly presenting our PFC with numerous issues and concerns.

When it comes to your prefrontal cortex, it prefers to work on a single task at a time. As you recall, the PFC has notable limitations when it comes to its ability to store information. Because it relies on working memory, its capacity to address multiple challenges at once diminishes as the number of issues grows. Thus, when it becomes distracted by internal thoughts or external stimuli, it becomes less adept at performing its executive cognitive functions. That means with more distractions, your PFC will be less effective in making decisions, solving problems, and interpreting complex situations. In other words, your PFC does not multitask very well despite popular misconceptions.

Your PFC prefers to operate in a serial manner rather than engaging in multiple tasks running in parallel at once. By focusing on one thing at a time, and seeing it through, your PFC can be quite effective. But today's environments often fail to allow for such indulgences. Many jobs require multitasking today, and we are constantly being bombarded with information that requires us acknowledge new data before we have had time to process the last piece of information. Despite these demands, however, your PFC prefers to process one thing at a time without distractions. One only has to appreciate the difficulties we face today with drivers who are texting while driving to see that this is true. If we really want our brains to function at their best, then avoiding excessive distractions and allowing ourselves to focus on one task at a time is important.

Let's conduct a little experiment to highlight this point. Using a stopwatch on your smartphone or watch, time yourself and record how long it takes for you to count from 1 to 10 as fast as you can. On average, most people are able to complete this task in 1.5 seconds. Next, repeat the same task, but this time, record how long it takes you to say alphabet letters sequentially from A to J. In this case, the average time for completion is usually 1.2 seconds. Therefore, the average time for both tasks performed sequentially would be around 2.7 seconds for most people. Now, perform one last task using your timer. As fast as you can, combine the numbers 1 through 10 with the letters A through J and recite them (i.e. 1-A, 2-B, 3-C, etc.). How long did this last task take? In all likelihood, it took longer than the other two tasks combined (2.7 seconds), and an inaccuracy likely occurred along the way.

The point of this experiment is to show that your PFC can perform quite efficiently and accurately when it's able to focus on one single task. But when it must combine two or more tasks, it tends to be less efficient and less accurate causing delays and making it more prone to errors. In essence, this is what happens when we ask our brains to multitask, and it also occurs when we allow external or internal distractions to interfere with whatever we are trying to process. If we truly want to be our best, then allowing our PFC to focus on one task at a time is essential. And this not only requires us to avoid multitasking as much as possible, but it also requires us to be present in the moment.

In addition to appreciating the limitations our PFC has in

multitasking, it is just as important to recognize that multiple thoughts can pose similar problems. Ruminating over past events and conversations can trigger active thoughts as well as emotions that affect our conscious thoughts. Likewise, anticipating future occurrences can also create current concerns that affect our attention and focus as well. In both of these instances, we are not truly living in the moment but instead dwelling on the past or anticipating the future. And in the process, we burden our PFC causing it to be less efficient and less accurate in managing the tasks that we need it to handle in the moment.

Being able to be consciously aware of the current moment and minimize past or future concerns will be discussed in greater detail later in this book. But for now, it is important to appreciate that these types of thought patterns hinder our PFC from properly performing its key roles. Just as external events and demands can cause major distractions and limit the PFC's abilities, so can internal thoughts and concerns. The more we can reduce these distractions, and the more we can allow our PFC to attend to one task at a time, the better it will be in guiding our decisions and choices throughout life.

CLOSE THOSE TABS! CONSERVE YOUR PFC ENERGY, AVOID BRAIN FOG

When it comes to teenage boys, there often seems to be no limit to their appetite. Between a high metabolism and the calories needed for growth, my son's perpetual hunger required frequent trips to the grocery store in order to keep the cupboard reasonably stocked. But even upon this backdrop of a voracious appetite, my son noticed one interesting thing. During the school week, despite eating a rather large breakfast, he would often be hungry by mid-morning. But on the weekends, he could eat a much smaller breakfast or skip breakfast altogether without the same thing occurring. Interestingly, this phenomenon can also be attributed to our PFC.

Whenever we are faced with learning a new task or devoting thoughts to a complex problem, we engage our PFC to help us out. But notably, our PFC is extremely **energy intensive**, and when it is stimulated, it requires fuel to keep it going. As a result, we naturally burn more calories and glucose when mentally stimulated, and this triggers an increase on our appetites. Being focused and investing a significant amount of our attention onto a specific task demands a good deal of energy, and unless glucose is around in adequate quantities, our PFC can quickly lose its ability to perform its main tasks.

Understanding that our PFC requires energy and fuel to properly function, it should also come as no surprise that our PFC tires easily when repeatedly challenge. For one, the capacity for our working memory to hold a tremendous amount of information at any given time is limited, and therefore, our PFC gets fatigued quickly when asked to perform complex tasks over and over again. This is also true when asked to complete several tasks at once or when you are tired or hungry. Just like a computer with too many browser windows open or with limited battery supply, information processing slows when our PFC is overwhelmed or has insufficient fuel.

Because of these features, our PFC tends to want to preserve its energy whenever possible. In fact, you may notice that your PFC can seem rather "lazy" at times. Have you ever gone to the grocery store in order to get a handful of items? If you have only 2 or 3 items to get, your ability to remember your grocery list is usually pretty good. Your PFC has no problem managing such a task. But as the number of items on your list increases, you task your PFC and its working memory to a greater extent. And eventually, you decide to make a written list to reduce the demands on your ability to recall all the items spontaneously. At first, this may feel like your PFC is simply being lazy, but in fact, it is simply trying to conserve energy and prevent itself from becoming over fatigued. In doing so, it preserves its ability to handle more challenging problems should they suddenly arise.

Whenever possible, your PFC would rather rely on stored information and memory so it doesn't have to work as hard. This allows your brain to conserve energy when possible, especially since our PFC is so energy intensive when asked to work. For example, suppose you were asked to perform a serial math challenge. You begin by multiplying 2 X 2, then 4 X 4, then 16 X 16, and finally 256 X 256. Naturally, the first few are easy enough and readily performed. But as the task becomes more complex, your PFC begins to look for energy-saving alternatives.

For most of us, this means we are pulling up the calculator app on our phones by the time we get to the third or fourth task.

All of this highlights the fact that our PFC requires a significant amount of energy to work effectively, and because energy reserves are limited, your PFC will try to conserve energy when it can. At the same time, this also explains that our PFC tires rather quickly with sustained attention and thinking. After 15 to 20 minutes of intense thought and focus, we become progressively more fatigued, and our ability to think and analyze problems starts to become less effective and efficient. Understanding this, you can start to appreciate why it's important to preserve your PFC for the more complex mental tasks at hand. By avoiding distractions, both internal and external, you permit your PFC to function more effectively. And in this way, you become better able to manage the challenges of any specific moment.

THE GATEKEEPER BETWEEN EMOTIONS AND ACTIONS

In addition to complex problem solving, focused attention, and constant assessment of your surroundings, the PFC is also quite adept in one other area... regulating your emotional reactions. Certainly, emotions are part of a normal response to many situations, and suppressing how you feel is not a strategy that is ever recommended. But expressing those emotions at the wrong time or allowing your reactions to be guided by emotions without the assistance of reason can be a nightmare. Fortunately, our PFC helps us regulate our emotions and better express them in the right way and at the right time.

Overall, the PFC is best at inhibiting some of our knee-jerk reactions that can often be triggered by the way we feel in the heat of the moment. For example, our PFC helps us refrain from lashing out at someone in anger before we have thought everything through. Likewise, it allows us to restrain ourselves before speaking our initial thoughts that might come to mind. And your PFC also inhibits specific types of behaviors. You can even thank your PFC for not eating the entire bag of chocolate chip cookies or tub of ice cream! In essence, your PFC is your guardian of reason and patience that encourages you to not react to your initial whims and desires but instead be more thoughtful and discerning before you decide to act.

In order to accomplish its regulatory function of your emotions, it has already been noted that your PFC needs to have adequate energy and fuel. Therefore, when you are stressed, tired, or drained of energy, you will more likely to lash out or react without necessarily thinking the situation over. The reason this occurs is not simply a lack of glucose and energy, however. It is also due to an imbalance of neurochemicals in the brain that can occur when you're overly stresses and fatigued. Your PFC requires **just the right levels of neurochemicals** to function properly, and in these instances, the right neurochemical balance is often lacking.

For this reason, the PFC has been referred to as the "Goldilocks of the brain." Levels of neurochemicals that are either too high or too low can interfere with your PFC's abilities. When emotions are running high, or your mood has been negatively affected, it's common for various neurochemicals like serotonin, dopamine, and norepinephrine to be imbalanced. Likewise, when stressed or reacting out of anxiety or fear, adrenaline and other neurochemical hormones can alter the PFC's function. Like Goldilocks, your PFC requires just the right balance of neurochemicals to perform tasks well.

Each of us has experienced circumstances where such a neurochemical imbalance may exist. Do you remember the last time you regretted something you said when in a heated argument? Do you recall a time when you felt like you simply couldn't think clearly because the moment was too overwhelming? In both of these situations, emotions and stress likely contributed to altered levels of neurochemicals, which in turn affected how well your PFC functioned. As a result, your ability to effectively regulate your emotions or problem solve was impaired. While these are not desirable behaviors, they can provide us with clues that we are experiencing excessive stress and poor emotional regulation.

Symptoms such as forgetfulness, lethargy, and distractibility are common when prefrontal fatigue is present. Likewise, ruminating over thoughts and situations as well as the inability to focus and complete various tasks are other frequent features of prefrontal cortex dysfunction. By appreciating these telltale signs, you can start to take steps to alleviate the situation. While maintaining the right neurochemical balance is challenging, it is not impossible. In fact, several strategies can be employed to help our PFC function at its best by ensuring it has the most favorable environments in which to perform. By understanding your PFC's role as well as its needs, you can be more conscious of various choices in your life that will allow your PFC to function well.

PREFRONTAL CORTEX SUMMARY POINTS

- The Prefrontal Cortex (PFC) represents the "CEO" of the brain

- Known as the executive or conscious brain, the PFC is responsible for assessing your surroundings and in key tasks like problem-solving and decision-making

- The PFC is the last part of your brain to develop and is the youngest part of the brain from an evolutionary perspective

- The PFC is located behind the forehead in the skull and is only 4-5 percent of your entire brain's mass

- Despite its importance in decision-making and problem-solving, the PFC has limited information and storage capacity

- Your PFC relies on working memory to perform its functions, which is limited and highly energy dependent

- Your PFC has 5 major functions which are:

  - Decision-making

  - Understanding and problem-solving

  - Short-term memorization

  - Information recall and processing

  - Emotional regulation and behavioral inhibition

- Information processing tends to be serial in nature with a preference to focus on one problem or issue at a time

- Your PFC has limited abilities to multitask and is not very effective in performing multiple tasks at once well

- Your PFC is easily distracted

- Your PFC is energy-intensive and requires fuel to optimally perform

- Your PFC prefers to conserve energy when possible giving it the appearance of being "lazy" at times

- Your PFC is also known as the "Goldilocks of the brain" because it requires the right balance of neurochemicals to function at its best

- Excessive stress, fatigue, and emotions can cause neurochemical imbalances that negatively affect PFC performance

LIMBIC SYSTEM

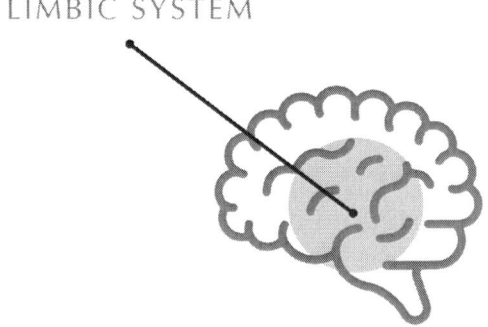

Behind The Scenes: The Limbic System

Your non-conscious brain is your operating system

Your limbic system is commonly referred to has your non-conscious brain. Unlike the prefrontal cortex, your limbic system operates in the background without you necessarily being aware that it's even active. In essence, your limbic system is your internal "operating system" just like the one that runs on your computer. You might be aware that you are typing or clicking commands into your computing device, but you don't see the actual internal operations carrying out those commands. In many ways, your limbic system can be thought of as being quite similar in nature.

At first, the idea that part of your brain is operating all on its own might be a little unnerving. But in actuality, your limbic system is what allows you to go through your daily routine on "auto-pilot." Unlike your prefrontal cortex, your limbic system has an enormous capacity to handle multiple tasks at once.

With relative ease, it is able to process, store, and retrieve a significant amount of information without us being aware. And in doing so, it frees up the rest of our brain to perform more complex tasks.

YOUR EMOTIONAL DATA CENTER

Many refer to the limbic system as the emotional center of our brains. As we learn new information and experience new events, your limbic system collects data and stores it away. But the data processed is not simply facts and figures. Instead, each piece of data also contains various emotions that we may have felt in relation to this information and our associated experience. And because of this, the limbic system is best able to participate in orchestrating our body's biological responses to various emotions. At a very basic level, this nonconscious part of our brains is able to encourage or discourage behaviors based on current and past events.

Let's consider an example to demonstrate how your limbic system operates. Suppose you were asked to stand up in front of a large group of people and make a speech. In terms of your prefrontal cortex, or your conscious brain, it would be aware of the steps that had to be taken to prepare and deliver the speech. But your limbic system reacts differently. It perceives threats of embarrassment, dislike by others, social judgment, and other related phenomenon at an unconscious level. These perceptions may be instinctual in nature, or they may be based on your past experience when speaking to large groups.

Regardless, all you know is that you feel nervous, anxious, and perhaps scared at the thought of giving the speech.

In essence, your limbic system serves as your emotional system, and because of this, it regulates many physical reactions within the body. Have you ever felt anxious or scared? If so, how did your physical body react? For most of us, our heart rate likely became increased, and we might have begun to perspire. Likewise, we likely became increasingly more aware of our surroundings as we begin to focus on specific concerns or threats we may anticipate. In some instances, we may not even know why we are feeling and reacting the way we are, but the phenomena occur all the same. In these types of situations, you can bet your limbic system is hard at work, interpreting your body's response to its environment.

The primary function of our brain is to keep us alive. It accomplishes this not by ensuring our hearts keep beating but instead by meeting our essential needs and protecting us from harm. For this reason, the brain is constantly looking for threats or rewards within our immediate environment. Specifically, your limbic system is the part of the brain that serve this role. As its fundamental operating principle, your limbic system repeatedly scans your surroundings looking for things that might potentially hurt you. And when things look or feel awry, it instructs us to focus our attention on the specific aspects of the situation that are most concerning.

At a very basic level, your limbic system is concerned about survival. From this perspective, your limbic system is involved in determining if you're about to be eaten or whether there is something available to eat. Likewise, one of its first inclinations is to assess whether someone is friend or foe. While these basic determinations are important, our world today demands much more from our limbic system. While lions, tigers, and other predators are not something we are likely to face, other threats exist. An angry boss, excessive traffic during your commute, and even an overflowing email inbox are more likely to be perceived threats today. These are the concerns that trigger our limbic system to jump into action in modern times.

While our limbic system is constantly looking for threats or potential rewards, it is important to appreciate that threats receive priority attention. In other words, your limbic system checks for potential harm first, and then checks things out for possible benefits. Because of this, we are often drawn toward negative stories as well as negative thinking to a greater extent. Because your limbic system pays more attention to threat, you will naturally be more focused on pieces of information that warn you about potentially bad outcomes and events. Likewise, by focusing on the negative aspects of a situation, we feel better prepared for some potential harm. All of this is your limbic system's doings.

While this may sound rather disheartening at first, there is some good news as well. Despite the fact that your limbic system is automatically geared to look for threats first, we can "retrain" our minds in the way it handles these responses. Specifically, we can acknowledge the potential threat, the negative story, and even our negative thoughts. But at the same time, we can choose to seek out the positive aspects and hopeful things associated with the situation. A committed effort toward these practices as well as an attitude of appreciation and gratitude are excellent tools to overcome these negative tendencies. And through practice, we can develop new neuropathways that help support these efforts progressively over time.

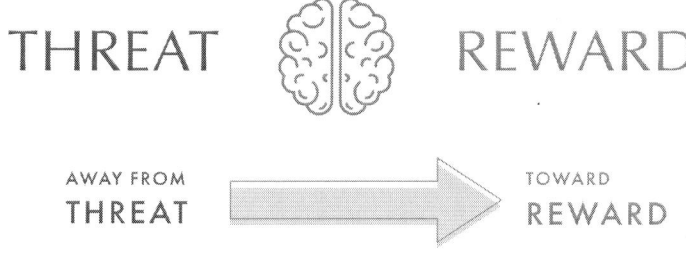

We move away from threat and toward reward.
Minimize danger, *Maximize* reward

In terms of the limbic system, one way to envision its structure is to think of it as "almonds" and "seahorses." On each side of the brain, your limbic system is composed of a left and right almond-shaped structure called the amygdala. Whenever we feel threatened or sense some type of reward, our amygdala becomes activated. Interestingly, research suggest that the right amygdala tends to be activated preferentially when we experience fear, anxiety, or sadness. But the left amygdala responds more to more positive emotions like happiness and pleasure. In essence, this suggests that threat and reward activate the amygdala on different sides of the brain.[15]

The amygdala function in conjunction with two other important structures of the limbic system called the hippocampi. You have a left and right hippocampus, which are the structures that are shaped more like seahorses. While the amygdala is primarily concerned with processing emotions, the hippocampi are more involved with storing memories. But because the hippocampi function alongside the amygdala, the memories stored not only record an experience but also the emotions associated with that experience. And as you might guess, the intensity of the emotions experienced for a specific memory is directly linked to the strength and impact that memory has on you at the time.

Consider this from a practical perspective. Do you remember where you were and what you were doing when the terrorist attacks occurred on September 11th, 2001? In all likelihood, you do. For me, I was driving to a prenatal office visit in Naples, Florida, excited to see the first image of my son by ultrasound when I heard the news. The intensity of the event, and the emotions it triggered, strongly etched that memory in my mind. But if you asked me where I was and what I was doing on September 11th any other year, I don't have the foggiest idea. This is how the amygdala and hippocampi work together linking emotions, memories, and their intensity together. And this all happens without us being aware of it.

The non-conscious nature of the limbic system is important to recognize. As part of its role in perceiving threat and reward, experiences associated with more intense emotions are kept "top of mind" and occupy a region of higher priority than less intense experiences. For this reason, intense memories that are emotionally charged are maintained long after the actual event. At the same time, the limbic system does not necessarily distinguish the difference between one memory and another that are similar in nature. Thus, you might experience the same emotions and reactions when two unrelated events share some features in common. Unless the nuances of these events are explored, it may be challenging to appreciate the connection. Because the limbic system operates without you being aware of it, these types of phenomena routinely occur without out us understanding why.

Imagine you were struck by another car from behind while driving along the highway. As with any car accident, your brain immediately shifts into high gear, so to speak. Your limbic system perceives an eminent threat and coordinates the biologic response associated with our fight, flight, or freeze mechanisms. As the driver gets out of the other vehicle and approaches you, you notice he is wearing a red sweater, has a thick beard, and smells like tobacco smoke. Though all of these details seem to be rather inconsequential at the time, your limbic system records each of them because of the heightened level of emotions associated with the accident. Yet, all the while, you may not even be aware that such details about the event have been stored inside your brain.

Months later, you are checking out at the grocery store. As the clerk rings up your items, you find yourself becoming a bit irritated with his behavior. Though he hasn't done anything wrong, you cannot help but feel somewhat angry at him. Interestingly enough, he just happens to be wearing a red sweater and boasts a pretty thick beard. And, his clothes have a slight smell of tobacco about them. The clerk hasn't done anything to threaten you in any way, but despite this, you experience a similar emotional reaction that you had during your car accident simply because of some noted similarities about the person. This is a perfect example of how our non-conscious limbic system operates.

REPATTERNING YOUR THREAT VS. REWARD RESPONSE

In many cases, our senses serve as triggers for these types of irrational or emotional responses. Sights, smells, sounds, and other sensations can stimulate our non-conscious brain to recall a variety of past memories, experiences, and emotions. One person I know realized that the sound of an emergency vehicle's siren was enough to change her attitude. After waking up refreshed and in a great mood, she suddenly found herself anxious and worried after returning from her morning walk to the coffee shop. After thinking about her walk, she realized a fire truck with its siren blaring had passed her. This noise had triggered her shift in mood because it was associated with a traumatic car accident she had been in when she was younger. By recognizing this association, she was fortunately able to consciously rationalize her anxiety away.

The limbic system serves to protect ourselves from harm, and whenever threat is perceived, it prepares us for fight, flight, or freeze. It's important to appreciate that each of these responses can be subtle in nature. For example, a fight response might appear as a minor irritation or frustration. Flight responses may encourage us to simply avoid an uncomfortable situation. And freezing responses could manifest as a disengagement or apparent lack of interest. Because of this, it can sometimes be difficult to see the limbic system at work. When the behaviors triggered by past experiences and their associated memories are less than profound, we often attribute them to other things. We may assume that we are just moody because of a lack of sleep or changes in our diet. And while this may be true at times, it is also common that these reactions a result of non-conscious memories that we fail to appreciate consciously.

Let's take another example for a past client of mine. Dave was known to be a highly achieving employee, and his work performance had been consistently superior in the past. But whenever he was confronted with a crisis, Dave would tend to "freeze up" and lose focus. The cause of Dave's reaction all stemmed from a learned behavior in his childhood. When Dave was young, his older sister had a tendency to dramatize every little issue and make it sound like an emergency. Dave learned to react to her behavior by retreating to his room in silence. In essence, his room was a safe-haven where he could escape the stress associated with his sister's reactions. This became a learned behavior prompted by his non-conscious brain. Thus, whenever Dave was faced with a crisis at work, he reverted to this same behavioral strategy and retreated into a state of inaction.

Fortunately, for Dave, he was able to break his existing pattern of behavior by acknowledging this tendency. In other words, by becoming more conscious of how his non-conscious limbic system drove his behaviors, he was able to choose a different response. With practice, he was then able to adopt a different approach to crisis situations and achieve his usual high level of performance. In essence, he was able to more effectively engage his prefrontal cortex in selecting how he should react rather than allowing his limbic system to be the primary guide. This is an important strategy to employ when we are dealing with behaviors motivated by emotional reactions and our non-conscious brain.

From these stories and discussions, you might get the impression that our limbic system prevents us from attaining our goals or undermines our best interests. But this couldn't be farther from the truth. Our limbic system is essential in helping us avoid threatening situations and environments. Fear and other emotions associated with perceived threats triggers inherent instincts and reactions when time to process information simply doesn't exist. You don't want to have to study an oncoming herd of elephants, an attacking mountain lion, or a poisonous snake in your path. You simply want to react as quickly as possible in order to avoid the threat and protect yourself. This is why your limbic system is vitally important.

As you can appreciate, fear is an important emotion that guides our non-conscious behaviors. Of course, today we are not routinely faced with wild animals and snakes, but that doesn't mean fear doesn't still drive our behavioral responses. In fact, some of the most common fears today involve situations and circumstances that trigger concerns about poor performance, our inadequacies, and our lack of being accepted. These instances often create a sense of fear that can then result in some type of fight, flight, or freeze response. But that doesn't mean that you cannot modify or change these reactions. By understanding how your brain works, you can better manage your brain by teaching yourself to have positive thoughts and emotions. This promotes the creation of new neuropathways that will reduce the influence that non-conscious fear has on your behaviors while promoting resilience at the same time.

WHAT YOU NEED TO KNOW ABOUT YOUR MEMORIES

When it comes to memories, the process by which we record and retrieve information and experiences is quite a mystery in many ways. For centuries, scientists and researchers have pondered how memory processes work. Yet, even with all the advances in technology today, the precise mechanisms that regulate our memory systems remain somewhat elusive. Likewise, many unusual patterns regarding memory formation and recall exist that are difficult to explain. In some instances, situations will be remembered in exquisite detail while others are not. In fact, research supports that some of the memories we form may be far from accurate, being influenced by the emotions, significance, and stress levels present at the time.

In addition to the effect that emotions have on our memories, some additional factors appear to create some degree of inconsistency when it comes to memory formation. It isn't unusual for aging individuals to forget details about events that occurred a few days previously or even that day. Yet, they can often recall intricate details of past events that might have occurred in their childhood. I have noticed this same phenomenon to some degree in my own memories. While I recall the precise colors, patterns, and placement of furniture of my grandparent's home when I was a child, this same level of detail escapes me when trying to remember homes that I have lived in later in my life.

Most of us appreciate how individuals will remember specific situations and circumstances differently. One person's perspective of a situation will be different from the next person's, and this causes facts to be stored and processed in different ways. Our past experiences, emotions, concerns, and prejudices all influence how we perceive things. And this affects how we catalog our memories of specific events. Many times, I have been at family gatherings where my relatives cannot agree on the specifics of some past event. And I am sure if you asked a group of your friends or family members about something that happened many years ago, each would remember it quite differently as well. Thus, while our memories are vitally important to our well-being, it must also be recognized that they are not always 100 percent accurate.

In the last section involving the prefrontal cortex, we talked about "working memory," which is used to process new incoming information. As mentioned, our working memory has limited capacity, and it cannot be bothered to guide many of our routine daily activities. These more routine behaviors are instead guided by the limbic system, which has tremendous mental capacity. Things like brushing your teeth, taking a shower, and making coffee are essentially activities we perform on "autopilot" thanks to our non-conscious limbic system. By tapping into those neuropathways previously created from past actions as well as past memories, your limbic system essentially "walks" you through the more mundane, routine tasks.

In this regard, memories play an important role in guiding our behaviors as does the brain structure responsible for creating these memories... the hippocampus. In essence, your hippocampus is responsible for processing and consolidating short-term memories and converting them into long-term ones. These types of memory formation activities actually cause your hippocampus to increase in size. As we learn and collect new memories, your hippocampus does more than simply serve as a cataloging center. Instead, your hippocampus is actually a "connection machine" that links memories together in an effort to help us attain learned concepts. Thus, your memories are not simply a tape-recording device of your past but actually a critical part of your ability to learn.

Regarding memories, some are considered explicit while other implicit. Explicit memories are those that require the conscious recall of information that you have learned previously. This involves the ability to retrieve facts and details about events, circumstances, and experiences. This is particularly useful when taking a test, remembering a shopping list, or trying to figure out where you left your car keys. Because explicit memories are conscious memories, these routinely involve the prefrontal cortex. Some explicit memories may already be present within your working memory. Or your prefrontal cortex may retrieve a stored memory into your conscious thought processes when it is relevant to the task at hand.

In contrast, implicit memories occur without conscious awareness. Without your knowing, implicit memories provide information stored from past experiences that can be used to perform a variety of activities. For example, implicit memories provide you with the ability to ride a bicycle, play a sport, or drive a car. Once these have been learned initially, implicit memories are retrieved to facilitate these actions over and over again. In fact, some implicit memories begin to be encoded within our brains while we are still an embryo in the womb. Referred to as "priming," these early encodings can affect how we respond to specific situations based on the implicit memories formed at the time.

A perfect example of how implicit memories can affect us even before our birth relates to my son's response to a particular song. During my pregnancy, I played the song, Pachelbel's Canon in D, repeatedly throughout the week, and I even played the song during his actual birth. Even today, many years later, my son has no conscious recollection of the song during his childhood. But the song consistently provides him with a sense of peacefulness and calmness when it is played. This type of implicit memory is called an associative memory because it links a feeling or belief to a specific event. Thus, despite my son having no conscious recall of the song early in his life, he continues to associate the song with a serene and safe environment.

Unlike unconscious memories that are repressed or inaccessible, implicit memories are in the forefront of our minds despite our lack of awareness of them. Dr. Dan Siegel, in his book, Mindset, provides a great story to showcase this point. In the story, a female patient with an inability to remember faces or names visits a neurologist on several occasions. With each encounter, the neurologist has to reintroduce himself to the woman and shake her hand. One day, however, the neurologist held a small pin in his hand that delivered an uncomfortable prick to the women as they shook hands, which she naturally found unpleasant. And while she still didn't remember the neurologist during subsequent visits, she would no longer shake his hand.[16]

The key point here is that implicit memories are quite important in triggering emotions, behaviors, and beliefs, even though we are completely unaware of them. Past experiences create memories within our limbic system that are rich with emotions and perceptions. These memories often guide our responses in many ways. But at the same time, we do have the ability to influence these reactions. For one, getting adequate rest and sleep is an important activity that facilitates more effective memory formation and conceptual learning. Likewise, mental reflection on past events and experiences forces us to retrieve past memories into our conscious brain. In doing so, we invite the opportunity to change how we perceive these memories. This is an important concept to appreciate since it will offer tremendous chances for positive growth and change in your life.

NON-CONSCIOUS EMOTIONS VS. CONSCIOUS FEELINGS

Can you imagine a life void of emotion? How would you know what had significance or meaning? Personally, I think that emotion is what makes us uniquely human. Emotions add value and meaning to what we learn, to our experiences of love and loss, and to every event in our lives. The experience of emotion provides us the opportunity to grow and evolve, expanding our understanding of self and others. Emotion allows us to feel. To feel grateful, empathic, and compassionate for others and to engage and connect with others through love. Thus, it is certainly important that we explore the role emotions serve in terms of our brain's functions.

Deep within your limbic system, emotions serve many important roles that enhance your well-being. For one, emotions provide cues guiding you to pay attention to potential threats or rewards. This may relate to events occurring in your immediate surroundings, or it may involve sensations and thoughts within your own body. Emotions also affect the decisions we make, for better or worse, by influencing how we perceive situations. Personal values, beliefs, and past experiences each have emotions attached to them, and these routinely play a part in the choices we make. For these reasons, it's important to appreciate the impact emotions play in our lives at any given moment.

The science of emotion continues to evolve in terms of how emotions are perceived. This includes the more longstanding classical view of emotion as well as a new emerging theory of constructed emotion. But regardless of how we perceive emotions, it is clear that specific regions of the brain do not correlate with specific emotions. Instead, networks of the brain regions "light up" when a particular emotion is experienced. Thus, when you experience a particular feeling, multiple areas of brain act together in unison to create the experience. Just as typing on a keyboard requires your brain, nerves, tendons, and muscles to coordinate their efforts together, emotions appear to occur as the result of a similar concerted level of activity.

In understanding how emotions have generally been viewed in the past, it is important to appreciate the classical theory of emotions. This perspective supports the notion that emotions are automatic, universal, and "hardwired" in our brains. In essence, the classical view assumes individuals react to threats and rewards in a similar fashion because emotional patterns are similar from one person to the next. In other words, it has been believed that fear was experienced in the same way for everyone because emotions are hardwired in everyone's brain from the start. And it would suggest that the same trigger should evoke the same emotional response across the board. While this rather simplistic view might initially seem reasonable, it fails to explain what occurs in reality. It is well appreciated that same threat might evoke a "fight" response in one person while causing another to "freeze." Given this, the construction of emotions must be more complex than the classical view would suggest.

A more recent theory that attempts to explain emotions is termed the Theory of Constructed Emotion. Neuroscientist Lisa Feldman Barrett has invested a significant amount of time in researching emotions and offered this alternative theory of emotions. In her proposed theory, emotions are not simply hardwired from birth into some categorical fight, flight, or freeze groups. Instead, emotions are created from a combination of inputs that involve your body, your memories, and your surrounding environment. In her book, How Emotions Are Made, Barrett explains that emotions evolve as a result of neural, social, and psychological influences. Memories of past experiences, various environmental inputs, and existing neuropathways all contribute to create feelings in the moment according to her theory.[17] This is notably different from classical emotion theory.

In conjunction with this Theory of Constructed Emotion, Barrett also challenges the belief that we can predict how someone else is feeling based on their facial expression, verbal tone, or other non-verbal cues. Certainly, these features are routinely used to evaluate how another person might be feeling at the time, and in many instances, they can be as effective as verbal communications in this regard. But likewise, these non-verbal expressions can be affected by past experiences, cultural factors, and our own perceptions. Thus, while someone may appear to be angry, upset, sad, or happy based on a facial expression or vocal tone, they may not be. Because emotions are believed to be constructed based on a variety of circumstances, not everyone's non-verbal expressions will necessarily be the same for a particular emotion.[18]

To some extent, our limited ability to predict another person's emotional state based on their expressions results from how we learned emotions as a child. Often called a priming effect, a facial expression is usually shown as part of a learning task. In short, a child is asked to link various expressions with a corresponding emotion. Ultimately, this "primes" our brains to connect specific expressions with specific emotions, which may at times be inaccurate. For individuals from different cultures, or with different learning experiences, a particular expression may not be associated with the emotion for which it is supposed to be linked. Because of the variability in our life experiences, we are not always able to accurately assess how someone else is feeling.

Misinterpreting someone's expressions as the wrong emotion is not uncommon, as this has actually happened to me on several occasions. For example, my son has thought that the look on my face was an expression of anger, but in reality, it was simply one of concern. Likewise, I have thought my husband was upset based on his appearance when he was simply focusing intently on a problem. These are examples that are subtle in nature, but they highlight how expressions are not always interpreted accurately. Likewise, they also support how each of us construct our emotions somewhat uniquely.

Emotions are your reactions to both external and internal phenomena. It's my experience (and a view supported by neuroscience research) that your brain and your body work together to create the emotions that you experience. From one perspective, your brain collects inputs from your internal body. Your brain is constantly monitoring the sensations within your body including those from your internal organs, skin, and various sensory receptors. At the same time, it is also monitoring changes in hormone levels, immune system function, and levels of fatigue. All of these internal sensations are interpreted as being pleasant or unpleasant, beneficial or detrimental. This process, known as *interoception*, plays an essential role in the creation of emotions. Depending on the way these internal perceptions are interpreted, your emotional state could potentially change.

The emotions we experience are ultimately a byproduct of these internal inputs that our brains receive. In this way, our brain and body work together to create the emotions present at any given time. However, there is an important distinction that must be made from a neuroscience point of view. Despite being frequently used interchangeably, there is a fundamental difference between emotions and feelings. In short, emotions result from the effects that neurochemicals (including hormones) have on our brains whereas feelings are the conscious experiences of these changes. In other words, emotions are more non-conscious while feelings are more conscious.

Understanding this distinction, it makes sense that emotions tend to be associated with our limbic system. Being non-conscious responses to neurochemical changes in the brain, emotions reside deep within our limbic system guiding automatic, non-conscious behaviors. And emotions have the ability to trigger physical reactions in response to specific stimuli. If we experience emotions of fear and anxiety, then our heart rate may increase, and we may begin to perspire. Yet, this does not necessarily mean we are consciously aware of our fear and anxiety. Sometimes, we simply experience an emotion at a non-conscious level while being consciously unaware of its presence or cause. This offers an example of how you may encounter an emotional response without experiencing any specific feeling whatsoever.

Feelings, on the other hand, are conscious in nature. Feelings result from an aware interpretation of our emotions. In other words, feelings are emotions that are being consciously appreciated and interpreted while non-feeling emotions remain below the surface. Another way to think of this is that emotions exist within our (non-conscious) limbic system, but feelings require the (conscious) prefrontal cortex in order become aware of them. Similar to our Iceberg Model, emotions can often exist below the surface without our awareness of them. But once we allow them to surface into our consciousness, we turn these emotions into actual feelings. Feelings are labels we assign to emotion.

Past experiences, memories, and interpretations of one's environment can all influence your interpretation of an emotion. Your brain is constantly scanning your environment to make connections, anticipate events, and perceive threats and rewards. Sights, sounds, smells and input from all your senses are analyzed based on these factors. Of course, these factors vary from one person to the next. And because of this, similar emotions may trigger different feelings in different individuals. This is one reason it is so important to explore your emotions and feelings in an effort to better know yourself.

Let's take an example to highlight the distinction between emotions and feelings. Imagine that you are on a rollercoaster with a friend and about to take that dive downwards. Both of your brains respond by releasing adrenaline, dopamine, and other neurochemicals. The emotional response that follows evokes bodily changes that are quite similar in you both. But based on your past experiences, memories, and other factors, you may feel excited while your friend feels terrified. The conscious awareness of the emotion in combination with other factors is what ultimately culminates in the way your actually feel. This explains why predicting how someone else feels is so difficult, and why it often requires constant self-reflection to better understand why you feel the way you do.

Your brain has a tremendous capacity to anticipate and predict what is about to occur. By tapping into past experiences, memories, and internal cues, it will attempt to predict what will happen next. And these predictions can be quite powerful in nature, triggering specific neurochemical changes and emotions to follow. In this way, thoughts and experiences can drive emotions to occur even before an event happens. For instance, thoughts of an old friend could stimulate emotions of joy or sadness depending on whether they focused on prior good times shared or remorse over not seeing them recently. This is important to recognize since this also offers opportunities for you to shift emotional reactions by shifting your own thoughts and perceptions.

This particular concept has had notable relevance in my own life. Once I realized my brain's propensity to predict and forecast events that were about to take place, it allowed me to reassess a number of situations. One of these involved the relationship I had with my mother. I discovered that the unpleasant emotions I was experiencing with my mother stemmed from prior interactions with her in the past. But these interactions had no relevance to my current relationship. My limbic system was attempting to protect me from an uncomfortable situation based on prior experiences. But in the process, it was perpetuating a negative encounter that simply was not justified. As a result of this new insight, I was able to change my thinking, and in turn, alter my emotional reaction and behavior. The result of this realization has been a much-improved relationship with my mother ever since.

In returning to the distinction between emotions and feelings, everyone has an innate capacity to experience emotions. The limbic system's tendency to predict and anticipate events as part of its threat and reward monitoring naturally evokes emotional reactions. In some regard, the classical or traditional view of emotions has relevance here. But when it comes to feelings, which are the conscious perceptions of our emotions, greater variability among individuals exist. Based on a number of factors, the feelings experienced can differ greatly from one person to the next, as can how these feelings are expressed. As a result, feelings align much better with the Theory of Constructed Emotion. Depending on how feelings are constructed determines how one will experience as well as express the emotions they encounter.

Among life experiences that affect emotional interpretations, family interactions as well as social and cultural influences play a major role. You likely appreciate that some people nervously laugh when they become scared, which can be certainly be interpreted the wrong way! Likewise, some people cry when they are happy while others will not. For me, the way my parents reacted when angry had a significant influence on how I expressed anger in later years. While my mother felt comfortable verbally expressing her anger, my father did not. Instead, he would tend to "clam up" and become quiet when upset. Ultimately, I adopted an expression of anger that was closer to my father's behaviors. Having seen this as an example of how anger might be expressed, I was influenced by these life experiences in my own unique emotional expressions thereafter.

Certainly, emotional expression varies based on life experiences and socio-cultural influences. But at the same time, our interpretations of others' emotional responses and reactions are also influenced by these events. For example, my parents separated and eventually divorced when I was around 6 years of age. In their own way, both expressed anger on several occasions in front of me during this time. And while it was not their intention to do so, I began to associated the emotion of anger with dislike. Subsequently, I would therefore interpret someone's anger as their disapproval of me as a person. Because I had come to connect anger with my parents' unhappy relationship, I interpreted all anger in this fashion. It was only later in life that I realized anger can also be an expression that someone cares deeply about you.

For many years, I often cried when I became angry, not realizing that I was actually experiencing anger at the time. Interestingly, this is a known psychological phenomenon that occurs in some children as they choose a more acceptable emotional response over a less acceptable one. Crying was a more reasonable expectation for a child based on social and cultural norms when compared to other expressions of anger. Therefore, I replaced yelling and screaming with crying in an effort to gain favor and perhaps attention from my parents. But I continued to cry as an adult when I became angry as well, since this was a learned behavior I had adopted. Once I realized this, I began to ask myself if I might be angry about something whenever I would feel like crying. As a result, this has allowed me to become more aware of my non-conscious emotional reactions so I might gain greater insight into my situation.

Emotions (as well as feelings, expressions, and interpretations) are complex brain phenomenon that have yet to be fully understood. But it is evident that the limbic system plays an important role in this regard and that greater insights about one's emotions can be gained by exposing non-conscious reactions to conscious awareness. At a foundational level, emotions serve to help protect us from harm and to attain the things we need to survive. But at the same time, emotions can also negatively affect our lives when they are poorly understood. It is for this reason that a better appreciation of emotions is needed so that they can be more effectively managed. In doing so, we allow ourselves the opportunity to be the best we can be.

MANAGING EMOTIONS

Sometimes our emotions "get the best of us." There are plenty of examples where emotions may run amuck leading to the loss of friendships, family relationships, spouses, jobs and even lives. We also hear the term "trigger" a lot when referring to an emotional reaction that appears to be automatic and without conscious control in expression. Of course, this is not exactly the case. Someone may not feel that they have reasonable control over their emotional reactions, but in reality, our brains have an extensive control network that enables us to override these reactions and choose more thoughtful, conscious behaviors. These mechanisms may not always prevent us from reacting the way we wish we had, but they do exist nonetheless.

All of us have experienced times where we said things that we wish we hadn't in the heat of the moment. In these instances, we allow our emotions to overwhelm us and guide our responses and behavior. But this doesn't have to be the case. While some individuals with brain injury or illness may lack this capacity, the vast majority of us are able to control our emotions and behaviors just as we can control our breathing and thoughts. Of course, this may be easier to accomplish in some situations more than others. But in every instance, we do enjoy an ability to regulate our emotional responses and reactions.

In terms of regulating your emotional reactions and behaviors, this should not be pursued by trying to suppress the emotions you are experiencing. In fact, when individuals try to suppress their emotions, research has shown that activity in the amygdala, our emotional centers, actually increases rather than decreases.[19] This means that suppression enhances emotional strength despite the fact that we keep it from our conscious awareness. This helps explain why some people may eventually "explode" after suppressing an intense emotion for a long period of time.

It is also noteworthy that changes occur in the prefrontal cortex when strong emotions are experienced. Specifically, the ability of the prefrontal cortex to regulate and inhibit knee-jerk emotional reactions is significantly reduced as the intensity of an emotion increases.[20] Therefore, it is important to "train" your prefrontal cortex by raising your level of awareness about the emotions you are experiencing. In doing so, you continually engage rational thinking and can alter your behavior in a more desirable manner. And by doing this repeatedly, you can create new neural pathways that facilitate better responses over time.

Emotions are not only the body's reaction to external events but to internal thinking as well. Change your thought patterns, and you can change your emotions. In fact, reframing and reassessing your feelings are powerful tools to help you achieve better emotional regulation. Consider someone driving by a church where dozens of people are gathered outside with a few crying. Anticipating that the emotional expressions are suggestive of a funeral, feelings of sadness and empathy begin to surface. But as it turns out, the gathering is actually a wedding where some are showing tears of joy. By reframing and reassessing the situation, a completely different set of feelings then emerge. Naturally, our limbic system wants to interpret situations based on past experiences and the most likely scenario. But by taking the time to reflect and consider other potential perspectives, we invite new interpretations that can completely change how we feel.

In addition to inviting new perspectives, other strategies can also be used to enhance the ability to control your emotions. Specifically, another excellent technique involves breathing. Think back when you were a child, and you had become upset about something. One of the first things your parents likely did was instruct you to take some deep breaths and relax. There is a reason this. For one, taking a deep breath will improve the amount of oxygen to your brain, but also, expanding your lungs triggers a parasympathetic reaction in your body. This means your heart rate slows and your brain releases endorphins, which are neurotransmitters that promote a natural calming effect. And the calmer you become, the more likely you can engage your prefrontal cortex to help you inhibit any unwanted behaviors or reactions.

Another way to reduce the intensity of your emotional reactions is to use a technique called labeling and relabeling. Labeling and relabeling refers to identifying an emotion you are experiencing and then reframing it using a more constructive term. For example, if you recognize you are experiencing worry and anxiety, you might relabel this as concern. Fear might be relabeled as anticipation. And anger could be relabeled as irritation or frustration. While this strategy may seem like it may be poorly effective, research suggests otherwise. In fact, studies show that when an emotion is consciously labeled, activity in the amygdala decreases and emotions become less intense.[21] As a result, the lower intensity permits the prefrontal cortex to better control any unwanted emotional reactions that might occur.

I recall a perfect example of how labeling and relabeling can help you control your emotions and associated responses to those emotions. A few years ago, I had prepared for a big presentation for a rather large audience. Though I was well prepared, I became increasingly nervous as the day of the presentation neared. My anxiety eventually got to the point that I doubted my ability to engage the audience and keep their attention. However, I chose to step back, take a deep breath, and define the emotion I was feeling. I then relabeled my nervousness as excitement, giving my feelings a more positive spin. Almost immediately, I felt better about the presentation and my abilities. I went from feeling anxious to excited, and the presentation went extremely well.

By relabeling emotions in a more positive manner, we are able to interrupt the feedback loop that leads to a vicious cycle of negative feelings. In Pema Chodron's book, *Living Beautifully with Uncertainty and Change*, she notes that a negative emotion that is triggered within our limbic system results in secondary changes in the autonomic system. This response can affect our heart rate, blood pressure, sweat glands, and other physiologic processes. But the important piece of information that she revealed is that this response only lasts 90 seconds or so. When the negative feelings last longer than this, it is because we have chosen to rekindle the emotion over and over again.[22] By continuing to dwell on these negative feelings in our thoughts, we provide them with fuel that allows them to persist. But by relabeling them as more positive feelings, we break the cycle and evoke positive changes.

Whether you realize it or not, rekindling negative feelings are extremely common. When I was a child, my mother insisted on me having a "pixie" haircut, which was a rather short hairstyle popularized by Disney's character of Tinkerbell at the time. I hated having short hair, however, and once I was old enough to voice my own preferences with greater autonomy, I refused to have my mother choose my hairstyle. While this should have resolved the situation, it didn't. For years after, well into my adulthood, my mother would frequently comment about my hair. And each time she did, I would engage in an inner dialogue in my mind about why she had to comment about my hair. Feelings of anger, frustration, resentment, and even low self-worth would result from these thoughts. Because I chose to continuously dwell on her comments, I perpetuated these negative feelings for many years long after they should have dissipated.

Without question, emotions and feelings are important, but in order to be our best, we must learn to effectively manage them on occasion. By invoking breathing techniques, labeling and relabeling negative emotions into positive ones, and choosing a more constructive thought pattern, we can invite positive feelings into our lives. Naturally, this requires us to be more self-aware and to explore how we react to various experiences and circumstances. But through these efforts, we realize our capacity to grow and become the person we want to be.

UNDERSTANDING HABITS AND HABITUAL THINKING

In terms of habits, the limbic system plays a central role. Whenever you initially perform some type of task or engage in a new activity, your prefrontal cortex is actively involved. It must learn the steps and actions needed to complete the activity, which involves conscious awareness. But once the same task or activity is repeated several times, much of the brain processes required are stored within your long-term memory, which resides within the hippocampi of the limbic system. As a result, the behavior and actions required to complete the task in the future become more automated operating on a more non-conscious level. This enhances our efficiency in performing a number of activities, and it frees up space for our prefrontal cortex to deal with other issues.

In essence, this is how habits are created. Of course, the term habit often has a negative connotation with people assuming we are referring to bad habit. Smoking tobacco, consuming too many sweets, and speaking over others' conversation might be some examples of bad habits. But good habits are also formed in this manner. For example, brushing your teeth is a good habit that you likely learned when you were very young. Interestingly, most people still brush their teeth in the manner they learned this task as a child. Whether you brush top to bottom, side to side, or some other way, you probably adopted this approach when you first learned the task. This is because the task was stored within your limbic system, and it is now an automated, non-conscious behavior. In fact, you can probably brush your teeth now while performing other unrelated tasks, such as picking out your attire for the day.

Various behaviors and activities are not the only habits that we have that are hardwired in our brains. Your thinking patterns are also habitual in nature as well. In fact, did you know that it's estimated that you have over 70,000 thoughts a day, and over 90 percent of these thoughts are the same? This is an important piece of information to ponder because of the effect this has on our daily lives. By continually thinking the same thoughts over and over again, our ability to change and grow is limited. Not only do we end up thinking the same thoughts repeatedly, but in the process, we feed the same emotions, feelings, and behaviors as well. Unless we bring these non-conscious thoughts into our conscious awareness, we become a prisoner of our own habits. Recently, I read an interesting study where the participants were given a choice between fresh versus stale popcorn to eat. Naturally, the vast majority preferred the freshly popped popcorn.

However, when the same participants were given popcorn while seated in a movie theatre, those given stale popcorn ate just as much as those with fresh popcorn. In other words, because they had developed a habit of eating popcorn while in a movie theatre, the quality of the popcorn didn't matter that much. This highlights how challenging it can be to overcome a habit and inhibit its occurrence. It requires conscious effort and commitment using our prefrontal cortex to suppress these habitual reactions. And in order to extinguish them completely, we must do this over and over again for a long period of time.

While getting rid of a habit can be difficult, it is not impossible. The key is to not simply attempt to inhibit the behavior altogether but instead to replace the habit with another behavior. For example, one wouldn't stop going to the movies to avoid eating stale popcorn. Instead, they would make an effort to eat a healthy snack while in the theatre instead of the popcorn. By consciously recognizing the habit and making the effort to change, you can eventually change the way you think and behave. In the process, you will not only adopt better habits, but you will also become more self-aware. And instead of allowing your limbic system to direct your behaviors and reactions, you will become much more engaged and in charge of your life.

SUMMARY OF THE LIMBIC SYSTEM

- The limbic system is considered the non-conscious part of our brain and can be thought of as our own internal operating system

- Unlike the prefrontal cortex, the limbic system has a tremendous capacity for storing memory and processing information

- The limbic system is involved in memory formation, learning, emotion formation, emotional responses, and automated behaviors/habits

- The limbic system is also tasked with protecting us from harm and ensuring our survival by minimizing threats and maximizing rewards

- The limbic system is constantly monitoring internal and external cues in an effort to predict and anticipate potential threats and rewards

- Interoception refers to the internal cues that the brain receives as part of its constant monitoring activity

- The limbic system is composed of 2 primary structures called the amygdala and hippocampi

- The amygdala are almond-shaped and are responsible for emotion formation in response to internal and external cues

- The hippocampi are seahorse-shaped and are responsible for memory formation, long-term memory storage, and conceptual learning through memory connections

- Stored memories are affected by emotions surrounding the memory and the intensity of the memory content

- Memories of events are highly individualized because of variations in perceptions, experiences, and priming effects

- Explicit memories are conscious memories and recall that allow active use of information by the prefrontal cortex

- Implicit memories are non-conscious memories that guide behavior at a more emotional level

- Emotions are different from feelings

- Emotions are neurochemical and neurohormonal phenomena located in the limbic system that trigger physiologic reactions and operate at a non-conscious level

- Feelings are conscious interpretations of emotions in the prefrontal cortex that can be influenced by thoughts and changes in perspectives

- The Theory of Constructed Emotions describes how emotions are influenced by experiences, memories, culture, social interactions, internal physiology, and environment in their construction

- Expression of emotions can be highly individualized with significant variance from one person to another

- Managing emotions requires a conscious effort to understand and shift perspectives in an effort to construct more positive feelings, thoughts and behaviors

- Strategies to manage emotions can include breathing techniques, the adoption of new thought patterns, and labeling/relabeling of emotions experienced

- Changing perspectives and thinking patterns is important in an effort to avoid rekindling of negative thinking and unwanted behaviors and habits

- Habits are automated behaviors stored within the limbic system that enhance activity efficiency and allow the prefrontal cortex to have more capacity

- Changing habits requires replacing unwanted habits with desired ones as well as a persistent and conscious awareness of the change being pursued

- We are not slaves to our emotions but instead can choose to adopt practices that enhance self-awareness and positivity

NOVELTY

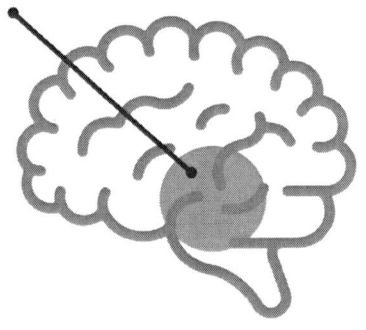

The Substantia Naigra-Ventral Tegmental Area

Your brain's novelty center and dopamine dealer

Are you drawn to the latest version of iPhone or Android? Perhaps, you are captivated by the most recent post on Twitter, LinkedIn, Snapchat or Facebook? Or maybe you have been obsessing over the newest model of your favorite brand of car? If any of these scenarios sound familiar, then you, like most everyone, are simply exploring what's new in your environment. Deep within your brain, your mind's novelty center is constantly on the lookout for anything new in your environment. After all, something new is exciting and intriguing, and novelty frequently deserves our attention so we can decide how to react and adapt. Your interest in the latest and newest happenings is not simply a fleeting desire. In fact, this passion for novelty contributes greatly to your ability to thrive.

Novelty is defined as anything new, original, or unusual. Anything novel naturally captures our brain's attention. This attraction to novelty motivates us to explore, to learn, and to discover everything that surrounds us. In fact, this is essential for our ability to survive as a species. Novelty is so important to our well-being that researchers have identified several health advantages that result from seeking new experiences in our lives. Specifically, exploring new activities and experiences improves our ability to learn while enhancing our memory. And these effects can have significant benefits in helping us achieve a healthier, happier, and longer life.

When you're exposed to something new that causes you to be excited or intrigued, your brain releases a chemical called dopamine. Dopamine is the chemical that creates a feeling of excitement and even euphoria. Researchers have found that a specific "novelty center" appears to exist in our brains.[23] Located deep in the brain in the Substantia Nigra and Ventral Tegmental Area (SN/VTA), the novelty center is stimulated when we experience something unexpected that is associated with a high level of emotions. When this happens, dopamine is released, which makes it likely we will perceive the experience as pleasing. And because the SN/VLA novelty center has important brain connections to learning and memory areas, these same experiences enhance our capacity to learn and grow.

The "rush" you receive from the release of dopamine is what links novelty to your desire to learn, your passion, and your personal growth. In fact, you need these new experiences in order to thrive and to realize your potential. If you no longer feel this rush of dopamine, you will likely give up on an activity and look for pleasure elsewhere. Career success is dependent on this, since you will become bored and unmotivated if new challenges are not sufficiently made available to you. Even your personal relationships will suffer if they are subject to predictable routines. For this reason, you should want to embrace novelty in all areas of your life.

Understanding this, it should also be appreciated that routines can negatively impact your willingness to invite novelty in your life. For example, I have always enjoyed traveling and have been on numerous trips throughout my life. But recently, I have been staying at home more for a variety of reasons. This past summer, I had the opportunity to travel to Italy on a last-minute adventure, and I was surprised to find myself feeling somewhat reluctant to leave the familiar comforts of my home. Fortunately, I realized this was simply a manifestation of my brain's tendency to find comfort and safety in the predictable rather than engaging in novel experiences. Understanding that this was my brain's reaction, and not my true heart's desire, allowed me to push though my hesitancy and pack my bags and go!

Our incessant curiosity about novel items and activities can drive us to achieve well beyond what we can imagine is possible. A great example of this involves Albert Einstein when he was just a small child. At the age of 5 years, Albert's father gave him a magnetic compass as a gift, which intrigued Albert immensely. As much as he would try, Albert couldn't "trick" his new toy into pointing in the wrong direction. Even after playing with the compass for hours, it continued to point to the true north. The novelty of the compass stimulated young Einstein's mind and subsequently drove Einstein to explore many other curiosities in the world of physics. Like Einstein, you have the same capacity to be curious about something new that in turn paves the way to some of your life's greatest achievements.

Novelty is what promotes innovation and drives your ability to create new solutions or inventions. In fact, without novel experiences, creativity and innovation are much less likely to flourish. Because your brain isn't challenged to consider new perspectives or to accept new information, your creative thinking stagnates. Without novelty that explores new insights and associations, your capacity to develop innovative ideas and solutions declines. In contrast, when you invite novelty into your life, your creativity and innovativeness expand. By embracing new experiences, you provide your brain with the necessary stimulation that fosters your creative genius to flourish.

While novelty, innovation, and creativity are important, a word of caution is necessary. As you may appreciate, a balance is needed when it comes to inviting novelty into your life. In the right amount, novelty offers many positive benefits. But if the novelty center of your brain is stimulated too often, it can create a state of anxiety or even lead to addiction-like behaviors. For example, if you scan Instagram, Tic Tok, Snap Chat, and

Facebook for long periods of time, or play video games for hours on end, a heightened sense of anxiety can follow. The persistent engagement in new information can create a fear that you might be missing out on something when you cease the activity. Likewise, when this area of your brain is stimulated too frequently, the potential for addiction-like behaviors may occur. Because dopamine makes you feel "good," your brain and body will seek to reproduce that sensation as it dissipates. Thus, the pursuit of novelty can become an obsessive activity rather than a constructive one in these instances. In such cases, novelty can become more of a distraction and detriment than the asset it should be.

DRIVEN TO DISTRACTION

One of the most telling signs that your novelty center is being overstimulated is that of distraction. When we are distracted, we are unable to focus our attention on important information, and as a result, this lack of attention prevents us from absorbing information well. For many of us, we are completely unaware that we are being affected by distractions until someone points it out to us. This may surface as forgetting to handle some type of task or responsibility, or it may involve not recalling a conversation that we had with someone. But as you can appreciate, if we fail to absorb the information from the start, it becomes impossible to store it in our memory banks. What looks like a memory problem is actually a problem of distraction and overstimulation of our novelty center.

In most cases, we are not even aware that we are overstimulating our novelty areas and becoming distracted. We may not think twice about watching television, checking social media, and trying to hold a conversation with someone all at the same time. Likewise, driving and texting is another behavior that is all too prevalent (as well as dangerous!). When we overstimulate our novelty center by these multitasking events, we divide our attention and invite distraction. And instead of focusing on one task or activity and doing it well, we end up performing all tasks rather poorly while increasing our potential for anxiety and obsessive behaviors. When we invite this type of distraction into our lives, we thus undermine our potential to be the best we can be.

Not too long ago, I was attending my son's baseball game. As I watched the game take place, I couldn't help but notice the coach repeatedly check his smart phone. Every half a minute or so, the coach would take his phone out of his pocket, check it, and then put it back. Without question, his ability to focus on the team as well as the game was limited as a result. And it was clear that he was obsessed with making sure he didn't miss some timely message on his phone. But in the process, he became completely ineffective in managing the tasks at hand. And in fact, I actually found myself completely distracted by his behavior being amazed at how often he reached into his pocket.

Of course, all of us are guilty of similar behaviors at times. In most instances, we are not even consciously aware that we are engaging in these distractions. As you may recall, our conscious prefrontal cortex has limited a capacity for processing information, and as a result, much of the new information we receive are being evaluated in our non-conscious limbic system. Thus, once we exhaust our prefrontal cortex through these types of distracting, multitasking activities, we begin to operate on a non-conscious level. And in the process, we lose the ability to focus our attention and effectively make rational choices. Instead, we increasingly operate on an emotional and reactive platform that can lead to anxiety, fear, and obsessive behaviors.

Recent research has shown that Americans engage in these types of distracting behaviors frequently. In fact, the average person in the U.S. checks their smart phone 96 times a day! That means we are checking these digital devices once every 10 minutes. And these habits are increasing. Based on similar research done 2 years prior, the frequency of checking our smart phones have increased by 20 percent.[24] The same applies to the use of social media. The average social media user spends about 2 hours and 16 minutes on social media each day.[25] Understanding that this usually involves intermittent, brief encounters, it is evident that this is another common distracting activity that many of us engage in today.

Unfortunately, our brains are being programed for distraction in today's world of technology. By being constantly connected to our smart phones, social media, and other technologies creates an ideal environment for distraction that prevents our ability to focus and concentrate. In fact, many apps and social media platforms are specifically designed with this in mind. They seek to constantly stimulate our novelty centers in an effort to create an addiction to the app or platform. But by pursuing this type of user manipulation, they cultivate a culture of distraction and inattention that is not in our best interest. The more we engage in these distracting behaviors, the less adept we are at focusing on the present moment.

This is not meant to imply that technology is the only distracting entity in our lives today, but it does play a progressively larger role compared to years past. In addition to these external distractions, we are also often affected by internal distractions as well. Common internal distractions include ruminating about past events or anticipating future occurrences. The more we dwell on the past and the future, the less aware we are of the present. For this reason, internal thoughts unrelated to the moment can similarly be distractions that make us less conscious. Just as external distractions can overload the conscious prefrontal cortex, so can internal distractions. And once overloaded, we become more likely to operate on "limbic autopilot," relying on patterned responses to guide us through our day.

As was discussed in the limbic system section, habits form when repeated behaviors or thoughts create well-established neuropathways. When it comes to distractions, both internal and external, these serve to increase our reliance on these habitual patterns because our prefrontal cortex becomes "maxed out" in dealing with them. This is why distracting behaviors and thoughts result in less rational choices and more emotionally reactive responses. But fortunately, this doesn't have to be the case. By understanding the role these distractions play in undermining our focus and decision-making, we can choose to "put on the brakes" and adopt better practices that enhance our attention, our focus, and ultimately, our well-being.

PUMP THE BREAKS, HIT PAUSE ON DISTRACTIONS

Without question, our brains have a strong attraction toward novelty. As noted, this attraction is important because it allows us to be aware of new developments in our environment that might need attention. But when novelty is excessive, and we allow our brains to become distracted by insignificant new information, we place ourselves at risk for poor choices, undesirable habits, and heightened anxieties. Fortunately, however, we have the ability to inhibit this attraction if we so choose. In fact, research now supports this simple fact.

Just like your car, your brain also has a set of brakes that allow us to refrain from seeking information novelty. Neuroscientist Matt Lieberman has performed extensive research in this area of neuroscience and has found that one specific region of our prefrontal cortex is associated with this **inhibition** behavior. Specifically, the right ventrolateral prefrontal cortex (VLPFC) is noted to have increased activity whenever self-regulatory behaviors occur. In other words, whenever we inhibit a motor, emotional, or thought response, the right VLPFC "lights up." For this reason, this area of our brain has been called its natural "braking system."

By engaging our brain's braking system, we can overcome the urge to check messages on social media, frequently pull out our smart phones, or participate in other forms of distracting behavior. Because the right VLPFC is part of our conscious prefrontal cortex, we can choose not to allow these behaviors or thought patterns to occur. In this regard, our ability to inhibit distractions is something we can freely choose to do. And while this might be considered an act of free will, each choice in this regard might be better described as a "free won't!"

Let's consider a common task used by neuroscientists to evaluate someone's capacity to engage their brains braking system. The test is called the "Stroop Color and Word Test," and it highlights how one must inhibit the brain's habitual response in order to perform the task accurately. In the test, subjects are asked to state the color of the letters of the word as quickly as possible. If the word happens to mean the same as its color, then the task is rapidly performed without difficulty. But if the word's meaning is different than its color, a delay occurs highlighting how the brain's knee-jerk reaction must be inhibited with a more conscious choice.[26] As an example, quickly read aloud the **colors** of the words below (and not the actual word itself):

a. Black

b. Grey

c. Grey

d. Black

The correct response is black, grey, black, grey. But commonly participants respond black, grey, grey, black as the brain wants to simply react to the word's spelling rather than its color. In order to complete the task properly, you have to engage your brain's braking system and consciously assess the actual color of the words. And the more you are able to use your brain's inhibition system, the better focus you tend to have in the moment. Rather than simply reacting at a non-conscious level, you force your conscious brain to attend to the present task at hand. And this is the key to managing distractions.

Managing distractions requires you inhibit reactions that occur at a nonconscious level. By pausing before responding to some type of stimulus, you activate better self-control in the process. This pause that is allowed between stimulus and response has been termed our "choice point." Our choice point provides us the space to engage our conscious mind, be aware of the present moment, and attend to what is truly important. In fact, finding this choice point is what allows us to gain better self-control in every aspect of our lives including our behaviors, decisions, thoughts, and emotional reactions.

ACHIEVING TRUE AWARENESS: MINDFULNESS VS. MIND-FULLNESS

Mindfulness means paying attention in a particular way; On purpose, in the present moment, and nonjudgmentally." - **Jon Kabat-Zinn, Founder - Mindfulness-Based Stress Reduction**[27]

When it comes to our choice point, the key to success is the ability to become aware. And in order to become aware, we must pay attention to what is happening in the present moment. Understanding this, you may at first assume that paying attention and having awareness are the same thing. But this is not the case. For example, if our attention is focused on past events or future developments, we are not likely very aware of the present to the fullest extent. Awareness does involve attention, but it requires us to focus our attention on the thoughts, behaviors, and emotions being experienced in the present. This is what allows us to make the best choices and decisions possible.

Your ability to operate at peak performance requires the capacity to observe your brain in action. In other words, being truly aware means being aware of your awareness! When we are able to perceive our current thoughts, feelings, emotions, and actions, we naturally bring these things into the light of consciousness. When we attain this level of awareness, then we are able to better engage our brain's braking system and make rational choices. But without this capacity, an opportunity for habitual reactions and emotions to take over and make decisions for us arises. Thus, the key is to develop your capacity to become increasingly aware in an effort to avoid these non-conscious reactions.

The dictionary defines **mindfulness** as a mental state achieved by focusing one's awareness on the present moment, while calmly acknowledging and accepting one's feelings, thoughts, and bodily sensations, used as a therapeutic technique.[28] In this regard, awareness can be appreciated as the ability to focus your attention on the present moment instead of on the past or the future. This facilitates mindfulness, which allows us to be less susceptible to distractions and less reactive in our responses. When our minds are "full" of distracting thoughts and actions, we become reactive in nature and less purposeful. But when we are mindful and can objectively observe these thoughts and action, we allow our conscious mind to respond in a much more rational way.

By focusing our attention on the present, we invite better awareness, mindfulness, and decision-making. But these efforts also require some degree of discernment of your present thoughts, actions, and emotions. While awareness should be accompanied by simple acceptance, it should also assess whether you are being truly attentive in all aspects. For example, you might be "in the moment" while repeatedly checking social media and emails, but you may be oblivious to other events occurring at the same time. As noted, our ability to be consciously aware is limited, and our susceptibility to distractions is noteworthy. Therefore, being aware and mindful requires us to be attentive and observant to everything happening and not just a few isolated events. This is possible when we are mindful and often impossible when our mind is full.

For these reasons, it's important to pay attention and observe the behaviors, feelings, and thoughts behind these in an effort to better understand ourselves. Behaviors result from a number of influences. While some may be genetic in nature, most are related to prior experiences and the interactions we have had with others. We naturally have a powerful survival instinct, which affects our thoughts, feelings, and behaviors. At the same time, our environment, social interactions, and previous experiences also influence our decisions and actions as well. Once you appreciate this fact, it becomes easier to recognize the "why" behind our thoughts, behaviors, and emotions. And this also contributes to a heightened level of self-awareness.

An important point to realize in this regard is the impact that social interactions have on the way we think, feel, and behave. Especially when we are young, we depend on others for our survival. But even as we grow older, the influence that others have on our lives is notable. Some effects may be constructive and positive while others are negative and destructive. But these social interactions and experiences affect our perspectives and the way we assess our environment. As we strive to become more aware and "in the moment," a greater appreciation of our thoughts, emotions and actions will occur. And at the same time, if we recognize how social experiences encouraged these effects, we invite an even deeper sense of self-awareness.

The following quote by George Burton Adams, famous historian and educator, highlights the impact social experiences have on our lives:

There is no such thing as a "self-made man".
We are made up of thousands of others.
Everyone who has ever done a kind deed for us,
or spoken one word of encouragement to us,
has entered into the makeup of our character and of our thoughts,
as well as our success.[29]

Of course, it can be challenging at times to appreciate the degree of influence these social interactions have on us. Let me provide a personal example. When I was a child, I became aware that my mother would become upset whenever I became disappointed, angry, or sad. On many occasions, she would tell me, "Don't feel that way," whenever I became upset. Naturally, she would say this in an effort to comfort me as well as alleviate her own discomfort, but her words also taught me to refrain from expressing my own feelings and emotions. This social experience with my mother thus significantly affected my thoughts and behaviors for many years until I had other social experiences that showed me how detrimental emotional inexpression could be.

These types of social interactions influence our behaviors, thoughts, and emotions because they tap into our need to survive. In terms of my mother, my survival instincts encouraged me to suppress my emotional expressions in an effort to appease my caretaker. Knowing I was dependent on her for survival as a young child, I naturally wanted to prevent her from becoming upset if possible. However, with later relationships as an adult, different social experiences showed me that emotional expression enhanced personal relationships. Knowing social supports and relationships were important for survival as an adult, I therefore learned to change how I thought and behaved in terms of expressing my feelings. As you can see, social interactions significantly influence what we think, how we feel, and how we behave.

In order to gain insights into these influences in our lives, heightened self-awareness is required. And pursuing mindfulness is an important step in this regard. Being mindful requires attention and awareness, and it requires unconditional acceptance of what is being observed. Rather than denying thoughts, behaviors, or emotions exist, accepting them for what they are allows us to better appreciate why we have adopted these patterns of thought and behavior. In turn, this will help us make better choices, attain a higher level of focus for the present, and avoid distractions that can get us off track.

For these reasons, the pursuit of mindfulness is important and necessary in allowing us to best utilize our brain's novelty center the way it should be.

Mindfulness is not meditation. Meditation is one of several tools that can support you in achieving mindfulness. Nor is mindfulness kindness, although mindfulness allows you to become a kinder person. Mindfulness is not concentration either. Concentration is to focus on something, while mindfulness is being aware. In a nutshell, mindfulness is being able to think about your thinking. And like all other skills, it takes time to develop, which is easier said than done. In addition to paying attention and becoming more aware, the practice of mindfulness requires motivation and effort as well as commitment and perseverance. For the brain to establish a "habit" of being mindful, it needs a well-traveled neuropathway. This means that you must repeat that behavior over and over again until it becomes a "natural" response. And through your commitment, dedication, and repeated practice toward this effort, mindfulness can be progressively enhanced.

From a personal perspective, the process of improving mindfulness in my life is a never-ending one. It is a lifelong practice that is inherently related to our humanness. Through mindfulness, we learn, evolve and grow mentally, emotionally and spiritually. However, it is very challenging to be "in the moment" with awareness of your thoughts on a continuous basis. For one, our prefrontal cortex is energy intensive and fatigues easily, which limits our capacity to be mindful all the time. And likewise, stress is an inevitable part of life that will affect your ability to pay attention and concentrate. But with continued effort and practice, your capacity for mindfulness will expand in time. And this is essential in your pursuit to attain your most important goals in life.

As your capacity to be mindful grows, you will gain increasing abilities to regulate your emotions and reactions by changing the way you think and perceive things. Thoughts that no longer serve you well can be eliminated. Likewise, you will gain a deeper appreciation of your own emotional triggers and how these relate to your existing thought patterns and behaviors. With an attitude of curiosity and a goal of simple observation, you will identify key insights into yourself and attain greater self-awareness. And subsequently, you can then choose to rewire these neuropathways into new thought patterns and behaviors that better serve you. This is the art of practicing self-directed neuroplasticity, and this reflects how mindfulness and self-awareness can dramatically change your life.

NOVELTY CENTER SUMMARY POINTS

- Your brain has a "novelty center" that is located in the Substantia Nigra/Ventral Tegmental Area (SN/VTA) deep in the brain

- Our brains are naturally inclined to attend to novel stimuli as this relates to survival instincts

- When we experience novelty, our SN/VTA releases dopamine, which provides a feeling of excitement and euphoria

- Novelty drives creativity and innovation and is important for human flourishing in the right amounts

- Novelty also plays a role in learning and memory

- In contrast, excessive novelty center stimulation can lead to anxiety as well as distractibility

- Distractions are everywhere, and the brain is very susceptible to them.

- Distractions eat up an average of 2.1 hours a day.

- Employees spend an average of 11 minutes on a project before being distracted.

- People switch activities every 3 minutes

- Information bombardment and multitasking are two types of external distractions that overstimulate our novelty center today

- Internal distractions also exist related to thoughts about past events and future predictions

- When our novelty center is overstimulated, our conscious prefrontal cortex becomes overloaded causing us to react to stimuli based on an automated nonconscious limbic system response

- Regulating your attention is the key to emotional regulation. It requires catching an impulse when it first emerges.

- We have the capacity to inhibit distractions by using our brain's braking system, which is located in the right ventrolateral prefrontal cortex (VLPFC)

- Self-control is a limited resource. Each time you stop yourself from doing something, the next impulse is harder to stop.

- Neuroscientists refer to this voluntary self-control and inhibition as "Free Won't"

- When we engage our VLPFC, we allow a space between stimulation and response for conscious decision-making, which is called the "choice point"

- The Stroop Color and Word Test can be used to assess and improve our ability to create choice points and enhance our brain's braking system

- Excessive distractions lead to our minds being "full" and habitual, non-conscious reactions rather than thoughtful, conscious responses

- Mindfulness is the practice of thinking about our thoughts, behaviors, and emotions in the present moment with an attitude of curiosity, observation, and acceptance

- Awareness invites mindfulness by being attentive to the present moment

- Self-awareness can also be enhanced by recognizing the impact social interactions have on the way we think, feel, and behave

- The practice of mindfulness requires commitment, effort, and perseverance and is a lifelong pursuit

- By practicing mindfulness, we engage the art of self-directed neuroplasticity that can improve our lives

Stress and the Brain

The stuff that weighs you down

Achieving and maintaining mindfulness is dependent upon continuous self-awareness and the awareness of others. Naturally, the awareness of others demands that we be present and mindful of our environment in addition to being empathetic. But self-awareness requires us to spend time self-reflecting. It also requires us to continuously assess our own thoughts, feelings, and reactions. Thus, in our pursuit of mindfulness, both internal and external awareness is important. Likewise, this awareness includes an appreciation of the effects that stress can have on our brain and our body.

High levels of stress wreak havoc with our ability to think rationally and our capacity to regulate our emotions. When stress levels are high, we become more reactionary and rely on instinct and learned behavior. As a result, we are often unable to come up with the best solutions and insights into a situation. We become distracted by worries and fears, which limits our capacity to be mindful. This is why it's important for us to appreciate the stressors we are experiencing and ways to effectively deal with these stressors.

We experience stress when we feel threatened. Threats are not new, and in fact, have been a part of our human experience for millennia. Threats have played a key role in our evolutionary progress, and interestingly, are even more prevalent today. We may no longer face lions, tigers, and other immediate threats to our lives, but others are just as substantial in terms of the stress response they create. Similarly, modern stressors occur much more frequently, which makes them much more likely to be a distraction to our mindfulness efforts.

Every day, most of us experience several events that raise our level of stress. From a global perspective, we experience changing economic conditions, threats of terrorism, and constant societal pressures. We are also exposed to media's fear-based reporting that not only drives their ratings but also our anxiety levels. Finally, each of us has our own personal stressors related to our jobs, our health, and the people for whom we care about. Because these stresses affect us significantly, it's important to appreciate how we perceive these stressors and how we react to them.

Statistics on stress reveal some profound insights about their effects. You might be surprised to find out that 75 to 90 percent of all doctors' office visits involve stress-related illnesses. Likewise, forty-three percent of all adults suffer adverse health effects from stress. Stress has been linked to a number of health conditions including headaches, high blood pressure, heart problems, and diabetes. Stress may also cause certain skin conditions, worsen asthma, and trigger depression, and anxiety. The Occupational Safety and Health Administration (OSHA) has declared stress a significant hazard of the workplace. According to their assessments, stress costs American industries over $300 billion annually in lost productivity.[30]

Stress is not only a problem for us living in the United States. Stress affects everyone across the globe. For instance, an alarming 91 percent of Australians describe feeling a significant amount of stress in their daily lives. In the United Kingdom, approximately 13.7 million working-days are lost due to stress-related illness at a cost of £28.3 billion per year.[31] And these statistics were collected well before the world began dealing with the COVID-19 pandemic.

Of course, the COVID-19 pandemic has been a game-changer when it comes to stress. Nearly everyone in the world has been affected by the pandemic. While many of us may not become infected with the virus, it will affect our lives regardless. From concerns about the wellbeing of ourselves and our loved ones, to the expansive economic and social threats we experience along the way, COVID-19 has increased everyone's level of stress. These reflect a natural stress response to a serious threat. But it also represents not only an individual stress reaction but a collective one as well involving the entire planet.

From a personal perspective, I have been observing my own

stress response to the pandemic. Naturally, I have concerns just like everyone else. My husband is a pilot with a major airline, so his risk of exposure is higher than many people's. Our son is completing his senior year online and faces many uncertainties regarding his freshman year in college this fall. Finally, my 97-year-old mother has been placed in lockdown in her assisted living facility. Yet despite all of this, I can't say that I feel overly afraid or anxious. I am, however, concerned, and I have found that with greater awareness, I can shift my mindset and identify the positive aspects of our changing environment. I have found that the fear-based messages from the media interfere the most with my ability to make this shift.

I have other family members, friends, and neighbors who are continuously engaged with social and traditional media sources and have a different reaction. They describe intense feelings of anxiety, sadness, and even anger at times in response to the pandemic and its associated restrictions. Though their life circumstances are quite similar, their reactions to the pandemic are different. They encounter and deal with this stress in a different way. Not only is this intriguing, but it is also revealing in relation to our brains' and bodies' stress response.

With this in mind, I will address many aspects of stress and its relationship to our wellbeing in this chapter. Without question, we each react differently to stress and experience unique stress effects along the way. But the human stress response also has many common features and common factors that tend to influence our responses. By better understanding stress in more detail, we can better appreciate how it can be managed. In doing so, we allow ourselves to be more mindful in our pursuits of total wellness.

"The brain is a tool which evolved to anticipate and overcome dangers, protect us from pain and to solve problems; so, dangers, pain and problems capture its attention."
- Rick Hanson, Psychologist and Author of Hardwiring Happiness[32]

THE HUMAN STRESS EXPERIENCE

As a term, we use the word stress in a variety of circumstances. We may describe our interactions with others as being stressful. For example, we might say, "That person is stressing me out." Or we may use stress to describe a general way we feel, such as when we say, "I am so stressed I can barely think." Though the insinuations are slightly different, both situations identify stress as something that is unpleasant and intense. Likewise, in both instances, we are commenting on a higher level of anxiety that the situations are causing. In this regard, these types of statements are describing more of our reaction to stress than defining stress specifically.

So, what exactly is stress? In terms of a specific definition, stress refers to a physiological response to any real or *perceived* threat or challenge. In other words, the threat or challenge that triggers stress does not necessarily have to exist. We only have to believe that it exists in order for us to experience stress.

When this type of situation occurs, we then respond to the threat or challenge at various levels. These levels include not only emotional ones but likewise physical and mental ones as well. The more threatened or challenged we feel, the more we will experience these stress effects.[33]

Perceiving stress plays an important role in human survival. Whether we are talking about prehistoric man recognizing dangers from wild beasts, or modern-day threats like pandemics, stress helps us prepare and anticipate what's next. We have basic survival instincts, and therefore, we are constantly on the lookout for dangers and threats. When we believe these types of situations are present, we trigger a stress response in our minds and bodies. It is this stress response that allows us to be best prepared for what's about to happen.

We routinely refer to the stress response as the "fight-flight-or-freeze" response. Depending on the situation, our stress response readies us to either defend ourselves, run away, or simply stay put. Each response reflects an important survival strategy. Thus, by stimulating the release of several different stress hormones, stress triggers a well-orchestrated response within our brains and bodies that best prepares us for what's to come.

You are probably quite familiar with a typical stress response. Think back to the last time you felt threatened or scared. In all likelihood, you could feel your heart pounding and your breath quicken. Your muscles may have become tense, and beads of sweat may have formed on your brow. Likewise, you were probably hyper-alert to the threat, focusing almost exclusively on it. The greater the threat the greater the tunnel vision. All of these things you experienced were part of your stress response, and in each case, they prepared you so that you could react quickly and effectively to survive the situation.

In most cases, your stress response is so instantaneous that its build-up is rarely evident. Despite this, quite a bit happens within our brains and bodies in these few split seconds. As we discussed in the section regarding our prefrontal cortex, our brains are constantly scanning our environment for potential threats (and rewards). Thus, this region and other parts of our brain's cortex are processing all sorts of inputs about our surroundings. Images, sounds, smells, and other sensations are collected and processed to assess whether potential dangers exist.

While our prefrontal cortex helps us assess a situation for danger, it may not respond quick enough in some instances. If you recall, our prefrontal cortex is limited in its information-processing abilities. This is where our amygdala comes into play. Located deep in the frontal part of our brain, our amygdala interprets sensory inputs and determines whether or not dangers might exist. In most cases, our amygdala in partnership with the hippocampus compares the current situation to past experiences to help make this determination.

Therefore, our amygdala spends little time "thinking" about the threat. Instead, it simply reacts and sounds the alarm if a threat is believed to exist.[34]

Once our amygdala determines a threat is potentially present, it sends a distress signal to the hypothalamus. Your hypothalamus is the part of your brain that regulates the release of many different hormones throughout the body. Thus, when the amygdala raises red flags, the hypothalamus coordinates a hormonal response that accounts for our fight-flight-freeze reaction, also known as the stress response. It is actually the release of these specific hormones that account for the way you feel when you are stressed.[35]

When it comes to your hypothalamus, it plays a central role in overseeing your autonomic nervous system response. Your autonomic nervous system is unique in that it controls many of the body's involuntary functions. For example, your breathing, your heart rate, and even your digestion is under nervous system control. But unlike voluntary systems that allow you to move your arm when you want, your autonomic nervous system controls these involuntary functions.

Understanding this, the autonomic nervous system has two parts… your sympathetic nervous system and your parasympathetic nervous system. When we are stressed, our sympathetic nervous system is activated by our hypothalamus. Think of the sympathetic nervous system like a gas pedal in your car. When it is stimulated, most things speed up. Our heart beats faster, our respirations increase, and our circulation moves blood to our muscles in case we need to act quickly. All of this occurs when the hypothalamus stimulates the sympathetic nervous system in response to a perceived threat.[36]

The main chemical that accounts for the immediate stress response is epinephrine, which is also known as adrenaline. As adrenaline circulates through the body, it has a powerful effect on sympathetic nerve receptors. Your senses become hyper-alert. Likewise, your circulation increases and the airways in your lungs widen. All of this results in more blood, glucose, and oxygen getting to your tissues, which improves your ability to respond to a potential threat. By stimulating the release of adrenaline, your hypothalamus can quickly prepare you for whatever reaction is needed.[37]

Your hypothalamus also oversees a very tightly controlled hormonal system in your body. The entire system is known as the HPA axis, which stands for the hypothalamus-pituitary-adrenal axis. In essence, once alerted by the amygdala, the hypothalamus stimulates your pituitary gland to make various substances. Some of these substances then stimulate your adrenal gland to produce hormones like cortisol. Where adrenalin is a rapid-response chemical to trigger an immediate stress response, cortisol is one that maintains the stress response for a longer period of time.[38]

Naturally, we don't want our stress response to last longer than it should. We want to identify a threat or danger, respond to it, and then return to a less stressful state. In this regard, our parasympathetic nervous slows everything down to facilitate this return to normal. In essence, our parasympathetic system serves as the *brake* to our stress response. But when these brakes are not working quite properly, we can run into some problems. In order to appreciate the types of problems we might encounter, it helps to understand the different types of stress that we often experience.[39]

TYPES OF STRESS

When it comes to stress, several different types may be described. For example, stress may be physical or psychological in nature. Physical stresses occur when we are asked to perform physical tasks above and beyond our abilities. This may occur in the presence of physical illness or disability, or it may result from excessive activity, fatigue, and/or a lack of sleep. In contrast, stress can also be psychological. Excessive worry, anxiety, and mental fatigue often accompany mental stress. Of course, these two types of stress can occur together, and in fact, often do. This is why people with some mental health conditions often have physical complaints as well.

While distinguishing physical and psychological stress types is helpful, it is also important to talk about acute versus chronic stress. When we experience acute stress, typically a situation develops quickly and the event is relatively short-lived. For example, preparing for a lecture in front of a large crowd may cause acute stress. But once the lecture is done, then the acute stress resolves. In contrast, chronic stress is more long-lasting and indurated. Someone who is caring for their aging parent with dementia for several years is likely to experience more chronic stress. While acute stresses may intermittently occur as well, like a fall, the pressures of caring for someone long-term better defines this stress as predominantly chronic.

Why is it important that we distinguish between acute and chronic stress? Mainly because they have significantly different effects on our well-being. When we experience acute stress, our stress response is limited to a short duration. While this may interfere with our ability to use reason and logic in the heat of the moment, it will not have other more lasting effects. In contrast, however, chronic stress is associated with many health risks. For example, heart disease, depression, gastrointestinal problems, infections, and even cancers become more likely in the presence of chronic stress.[40] Thus, it is essential that we identify factors causing our stress and take steps to resolve these so that total wellness can be better pursued.

Finally, stress can also be real or imagined. What do I mean by this? Consider the following example. Suppose you suddenly lost your job and had no immediate means of income. You had little savings, and you feared you would be unable to pay your rent and put food on the table. That is definitely a real stress. Now, suppose you thought your boss didn't like you and was going to fire you in the near future. You had no proof of this, and likewise, you weren't sure he disliked you. But regardless, you feared you would be in a similar situation without rent money or food. While this could turn out to be a real stress, it is simply an imagined or perceived threat at the current moment.

Believe it or not, a perceived or imagined stress can be just as powerful as a real stress. Because your brain and body respond in the exactly the same way to these types of stresses, the results can be identical. Both can lead to physical and psychological stress. Both can also cause acute and chronic types of stress. However, the key difference between the two is whether they are founded in fact or not. When we are overly anxious, lack self-confidence, or fail to know ourselves well, perceived threats can creep into our life and trigger imagined stress when it shouldn't. Certainly, some imagined threats may be worth considering, but all too often, we should simply acknowledge their presence and let them go. In order to do so, we need to appreciate what tends to cause these imagined stresses in our lives.

FACTORS CAUSING STRESS

When I was in my early 30s, I began to having pain in my stomach. After my doctor evaluated me, he informed me that I was suffering from excessive stress. Upon hearing this, I felt both confused and frustrated. Did he not believe that my discomfort was real? How could this be stress? At the time, I believed I was in excellent health. I was training for the New

York City Marathon, eating healthy foods, and other than my stomach, I had no issues. But as I began to examine my life, I soon realized I was over-extending myself. This, in addition to several life events at the time, ended up being the root cause of my problems.

In addition to the physical demands I had placed on my body, I had set lofty goals for my career pursuits as well. Being a high-achiever, I refused to accept failure as an option and was working excessively long hours as a result. Likewise, I was recently divorced, had changed employers, and had just moved from Atlanta to Charlotte, leaving behind many friends in the process. In short, I had experienced three of life's most major stressors in a short period of time while placing additional demands on myself to perform. It was clearly a recipe for a stress disaster.

My situation was not an unusual one. Many times, stress manifests itself in ways that we may not expect. For me, stress caused me to have stomach issues. For others, it might cause insomnia, muscle aches, or a variety of other symptoms. But as was evident in my situation, an array of factors had contributed to my stress-related condition. Some of these resulted from life circumstances. But others had been my own doing. The pressures I placed on myself and my own thoughts and expectations contributed greatly to the stress I was experiencing. Not only had my stress become excessive because of external factors, but internal triggers had similarly played a role. Thus, when it comes to assessing the factors in your life causing your stress, it is important to consider both life events as well as your own thoughts and feelings.

You will periodically experience several life events that are known to cause stress. Major ones are well known and can include things like divorce, dealing with an illness, relocating, changing jobs, losing a loved one, or filing bankruptcy. These types of experiences, and others, represent external factors that can trigger a stress response. Why? Because each of these situations pose their own set of threats that we must address. Relationships, employment, health, finances, as well as food, shelter, and clothing affect our livelihood and quality of life. Thus, it's no surprise that issues affecting these areas can cause us to feel a greater degree of stress.

External factors that can trigger a stress response are not things that we can control in most circumstances. However, we can control how we react to them. Our own emotional reactions, thoughts, and behaviors represent another source of stress that is more internal in nature. If we allow ourselves to obsess over life's circumstances, our stress level can build as well. Likewise, excessive worry, fears, and anxieties similarly cause higher degrees of stress. Therefore, we need to recognize the internal factors that may be causing our stress to increase as well. And at the same time, we should appreciate that we can actually reduce our stress by choosing to change how we react and think.

HOW YOUR BRAIN REACTS TO GOOD STRESS VS. BAD STRESS

In order to appreciate how stress affects us, we must understand its effects on our arousal system and our level of performance. Despite its negative connotation, stress is not always a bad thing. In fact, it can serve as a motivation to do our best, perform at our peak level, and achieve goals we didn't think were possible. The problem is that stress can also be excessive leading to the opposite effect. Therefore, it is essential that we understand that point where stress stops being beneficial and instead becomes a detriment.

Think back to a time when you were about to start a new job. The night before your first day, you were likely a bit nervous. You wanted to perform well, and you wanted to impress others around you. In your anticipation, you felt a degree of stress knowing that there was a chance you might not do as well as expected. So, you made sure your alarm was set, you got adequate sleep, and you reviewed the tasks you had been assigned to do. As a result, you made it through your first day on the job well.

In this situation, the stress you felt motivated you to prepare and excel in your new position. In essence, it enabled you to perform at your best ability, and in the process, it made you feel energized and engaged. This type of stress is beneficial stress, and we experience this form of stress in many activities and situations throughout life. Whether a new job, a new school, or a new life role, this level of stress allows us to rise to the occasion and successfully perform.

Unfortunately, stress doesn't always know when to stop. In some situation, we experience excessive amounts of stress, or we feel stress for long amounts of time. In both instances, we still experience a high level of arousal and motivation to do well. But when excessive, in degree or duration, stress can start to undermine our ability to perform. Rather than encouraging us to stay within our limits, excessive stress pushes us past our capacity into a danger zone. And ultimately, this can lead to complete exhaustion and diminish our ability to be healthy.

An excessive level of stress can be self-induced, or it may occur by chance. For example, marathon runners can experience excessive physical stress from over-training. As a result, they can no longer perform at their peak and end up being completely exhausted. Likewise, excessive stress can be experienced when you lose a loved one and face the challenge of moving forward in life alone. In this situation, stress can be paralyzing and once again cause you to struggle and feel completely depleted of energy.

Understanding this delicate balance between good stress and bad stress, researchers have developed models that show these effects graphically. Yerkes and Dodson describe these stress effects as part of a theory that plots performance against arousal in relation to varying levels of stress. The resulting "inverted-U" graph highlights how these parameters change as stress becomes excessive. In essence, we move from a productive, challenged state to a hyper-reactive, exhausted state as stress levels climb.[41] The goal of course is to find that perfect in-between stage where we enjoy optimal performance. But sometimes, this can be quite challenging.

The graph shown demonstrates the classic inverted-U shape of our stress curve as it relates to arousal and performance. But it's worth noting that this curve could represent the effect of stress over the course of many days as well as within a single day itself. For example, you may start out refreshed and well-rested. But as your day proceeds, various responsibilities related to family, job, and life slowly mount and tip you over your peak level of performance. Thus, by the time nighttime arrives, you are hyper-reactive and stressed and no longer capable of performing well. This might lead you to forego your evening workout routine, or it may cause you to get into an argument with your partner.

The degree of stress that allows us to perform at our best varies from one person to the next. Some individuals are more susceptible to the effects of stress based on their age, genetics, past experiences, and environment. What might be stressful to one person won't be to the next. Because of this, your stress curve will look different from someone else's. However, in every instance, the same inverted-U shape will be present. In other words, at some point, all of us are vulnerable to the effects of excessive stress.

IMPACT OF STRESS

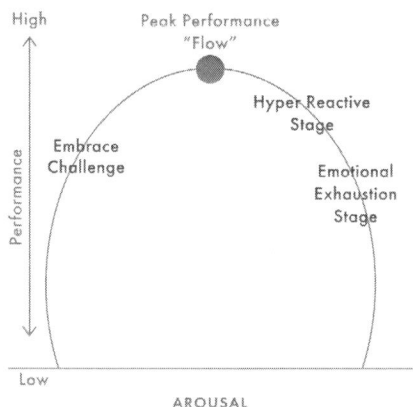

TELL-TALE SIGNS OF ONGOING OR EXCESSIVE STRESS

The right amount of stress can serve to improve our capacity to perform in specific situations where too much stress may undermine our abilities. At the same time, stress may also hinder our success when it lasts too long. For example, many athletes training for endurance events can place too much pressure on themselves to train and succeed. As a result, they overextend themselves physically, mentally, and even emotionally triggering a more chronic stress response. Instead of this stress response enhancing their results, it actually makes them less likely to achieve their goals.

The delicate balance between stress and performance is worth noting, and it's similarly important to recognize some of the tell-tale signs of excessive stress. Interestingly, you may be experiencing excessive or prolonged stress and not even realize it. This was certainly my situation when I began having stomach pains. Because many stress effects are subtle in their early stages, we may fail to appreciate the pressure we are under. And if this pressure continues without us knowing, a number of signs and symptoms can develop leading to poor performance as well as poor health.

One of the most common symptoms that may indicate chronic stress is fatigue. If you find yourself reaching for that extra cup of coffee or energy drink in the afternoon or evening, you might be experiencing the fatigue often associated with chronic stress. Some people use exercise to stimulate themselves in an effort to overcome these feelings of tiredness. But in both cases, the choice to take a stimulant or push yourself harder physically may only cause more fatigue down the road if your fatigue is due to excessive stress. Being aware of how you fatigue evolves over time can help provide clues about its potential relationship to stress.

Of course, fatigue is rather non-specific and can be due to other factors besides stress. Lack of sleep, poor diet, and other causes of fatigue exist. But chronic stress is a common cause of fatigue. When we are under chronic stress, our adrenal glands become over-stimulated, and eventually, the prolonged production of cortisol and other stress hormones from our adrenals begin to take a toll on our bodies. Not only does this result in fatigue, but this also causes us to be more susceptible to illness as our immune system becomes compromised. This is why chronic stress may also bring about frequent colds and infections, which may be another indication that stress is wearing you down.[42]

Overall, warning signs and symptoms related to excessive stress manifest themselves in three areas... *physical, mental, and emotional.* In terms of physical features, fatigue and infections have already been mentioned. But other physical complaints can also include headaches, stomach pain, insomnia, and pains and aches involving the joints and muscles. Some people may also experience chest pain or a racing heart beat when overly stressed. And still others describe digestive problems, loss of libido, and other unusual body sensations.[43] Naturally, the nonspecific nature of many of these symptoms can make it difficult to know whether stress is playing a part or not. But you should routinely consider stress as a culprit when other explanations are lacking.

It's probably not surprising that stress also causes cognitive and mental difficulties. Given that much of our stress response occurs in the brain, mental symptoms are to be expected. In this regard, stress can often result in a lack of mental energy. This causes us to process things more slowly and to become frustrated when confronted with complex information. Stress can also affect our concentration abilities, which in turn, makes us appear as if we are increasingly forgetful. And naturally, stress tends to push us toward our hyper-reactive side, which means we may experience racing thoughts and disorganized thinking.[44] Once again, these symptoms are rather nonspecific, but they also commonly occur with excessive stress.

Lastly, ongoing or excessive stress can also cause emotional symptoms. Most people are aware that constant worry and anxiety are manifestations of too much stress. But when stress persists for long periods of time, it can also lead to depression as well. Some people become quite moody when they experience high levels of stress, going from happy one minute to angry the next. Their stress causes them to be overly dependent on their circumstances from moment to moment. Thus, instead of being more even in their mood, they allow themselves to become hyper-reactive to their environment. All of this can lead to other emotional problems like low self-esteem, social isolation, and emotional despair unless properly addressed.[45]

As stress increases, any of these symptoms mentioned may develop. At the same time, you may notice that you begin adopting different behaviors in an effort to cope with your stress. For example, you may find that you are avoiding situations or people in an effort to protect yourself. Likewise, you might start biting your nails, fidgeting, or pacing around the room without realizing it. And for many people under tremendous stress, substance use becomes a problem. Tobacco, alcohol, and other prescription and illicit drugs may be used to help relieve some of the symptoms associated with excess stress. If any of these tell-tale signs exist, then you should strongly consider taking a look at the amount of stress you are experiencing.

THE LONG-TERM EFFECTS OF STRESS

Your body's stress response isn't a bad thing... necessarily. In fact, the stress response we have allows us to deal with stress effectively in most situations. Once the threat or concern has been addressed, then our stress response diminishes, and we return to our normal baseline. Unfortunately, however, stress can also become chronic, which is never ideal. Our brains and bodies were not meant to adopt stress as an ongoing lifestyle. Thus, when stress becomes too frequent or chronic, long-term consequences occur that undermine our wellbeing.

As mentioned, one of the key hormones associated with our stress response is cortisol. Cortisol is a glucocorticoid that has many beneficial effects in regulating a stress response. In moderation, cortisol is perfectly normal and healthy. In addition to restoring balance to the body after a stress event, cortisol plays a role in regulating blood sugar levels in cells and helps our brain's hippocampus process and store memories.[46] But it is also a "Goldilocks" compound. While the right amount promotes health and wellness, too little or too much can be detrimental. When cortisol is released in the correct amount, we are able to function at our best. The hormone makes sure enough glucose is available to meet the energy needs of our brain and body. Likewise, it also enhances our ability to process information.

And cortisol is also involved in reducing inflammation in the body. By reducing the amount of inflammatory proteins released by certain cells, cortisol protects our bodies from injury that might otherwise occur from an excessive immune response.[47]

Unfortunately, when we are under excessive amounts of stress, we may be exposed to prolonged amounts of cortisol. When this occurs, cortisol can actually undermine our health and wellness. For example, excess cortisol has been linked to heightened risks for diabetes and heart disease. It can also lead to chronic fatigue, sleep problems, and exhaustion. Our digestive, reproductive, and immune systems are negatively affected over time when too much cortisol is being produced. Recent research even shows that excess cortisol can promote obesity by stimulating our appetite, increasing fatty tissue, and lowering our energy levels.

With normal stress, cortisol helps us address any real threats successfully in the short-term and then allows us to return to a balanced, peaceful state. However, persistent and frequent release of cortisol can actually upset this balance over time. This is especially true within the brain. With excessive stress, your amygdala, hypothalamus and deeper areas are stimulated, which leaves less available energy for your prefrontal cortex. As a result, you are less adept at more complex, rational decision-making because your brain is constantly in survival mode.[49]
In addition to limiting our capacity for rational decision-making,

constant stress also impairs our ability to store memories. Stress reduces our ability to concentrate as we become more focused on potential threats. And with reduced concentration, we are less able to pay attention to details and store these details in our memory banks. Likewise, we also might have difficulty remembering pieces of information we should know when we are chronically stressed. Here again, stress shifts the action to other parts of our brains making it more difficult for us to retrieve information from our memory.[50]

I can certainly relate to these types of situations when stressed. For example, I have searched all over for my glasses only to later find them on top of my head. Likewise, I have been embarrassed when unable to think of someone's name who I have known for years. My first thought was that I might be having early dementia! But this was not the case. Instead, I was simply too stressed, and this affected my ability to pay attention and concentrate. Though it seemed like my memory was failing, it was actually stress that was interfering with my ability to focus.

Chronic stress has been identified as a major epidemic of our time. We may not be threatened with wild animals in life and death situations today. But the stresses we face can be substantial. From work deadlines, to family problems, to health issues, and more, stress can affect many areas of our lives. When we allow such stress to persist and build, it soon begins to undermine our wellbeing. This not only affects our ability to problem-solve and think, but it also impacts nearly every organ system in the body. This is why managing long-term stress effectively is so important.

NEUROPLASTICITY AND ACHIEVING STRESS RESILIENCE

Understanding that chronic stress has significant effects on the brain and body, it is also worthwhile noting how these effects can vary with age. At different stages of development, we become more or less vulnerable to the effects of stress. To put it another way, we are more or less resilient in our ability to tolerate and overcome the negative effects of stress at different ages. Certainly, stress can impose undesirable effects at any age if it is intense and prolonged enough. But the degree we are affected by stress definitely varies over the course of our lives.[51]

For example, research has shown recently that mothers experiencing significant stress while pregnant are more likely to have newborns with problems. Likewise, young children in their first years of development are also prone to emotional, behavioral, and cognitive problems when exposed to intense stress. In contrast, older children are more resilient as are individuals between the ages of 20 to 40 years. Yet, older individuals show less resilience to stress beyond this age range. Therefore, it is not only the degree and duration of stress we experience that can lead to problems. The resilience to stress also depends on our stage of development at the time.[52]

So, what causes this variability in our tolerance to stress? Some researchers have suggested that hormonal fluctuations may account for this in part. Specifically, higher amounts of gonadal hormones appear to increase our vulnerability to stress. In women, these types of hormones increase during pregnancy and around menopause. Thus, this may account for some of the variability.[53] However, it is more likely that neuroplasticity plays a larger role in our changing resilience to stress. It is well known that neuroplasticity in the brain gradually declines with age. Therefore, lower levels of resilience to stress may result from less robust neuroplasticity mechanisms. Therefore, we may be able to better protect ourselves from the negative effects of stress if we can boost our brain's neuroplasticity abilities.[54]

There is evidence that our brains do evolve and change when exposed to chronic stress. Specifically, stress has been shown to increase the size of the amygdala and hippocampus while shrinking the size of the prefrontal cortex. This makes sense since stress naturally stimulates these deeper brain regions when threats are perceived. Thus, it is likely that stress "rewires" our brains to augment the fight-flight-freeze response areas.[55] Our ability to be more resilient to stress is likely affected by these stress-induced neuroplasticity changes. But this is not necessarily a good thing. Certainly, we want to be resilient and respond to stress well. But with chronic stress, we may come to rely too heavily on our emotions and instincts. Rather than making more rational choices guided by our prefrontal cortex, we instead make rash decisions that may not be in our best interest. This can then lead to more stress and a vicious cycle of stress-induced decision-making.

On the one hand, we want to cultivate resilience in response to stress. But at the same time, we don't want to get ourselves into a chronic stress state. Because of this, it is important that we promote resilience while keeping stress in check. Fortunately, several strategies can be used in this regard. Physical exercise, socializing, and self-reflection are a few of these strategies that can help accomplish this. And no matter what age we are, we can use these techniques to achieve these stress resilience goals.[56]

A MODEL FOR CHECKING YOUR STRESS

When we react to stress through our fight-flight-freeze response, we are often described as using our instinctual brain. In other words, stress causes us to revert back to using the most primitive parts of our brain to respond to threats. But fortunately, our brains have evolved beyond instincts. Over time, the human brain has developed a highly functioning cerebral cortex that includes our prefrontal area. Because of this, we have a much greater capacity to not only assess the threats present but also control our reaction to them.

With this in mind, it is worth revisiting the Iceberg Model that was previously introduced. As you recall, our thoughts and feelings lie underneath the surface while our behaviors and reactions are available for all to see. Likewise, the model also shows how our thoughts guide our feelings, and therefore, it is possible that we can change how we feel by changing how we think about something. Thus, if we wish to obtain greater control over our lives, we simply need to reevaluate our thoughts and change them accordingly.

While this has relevance in many areas of wellness, it is

ICEBERG MODEL

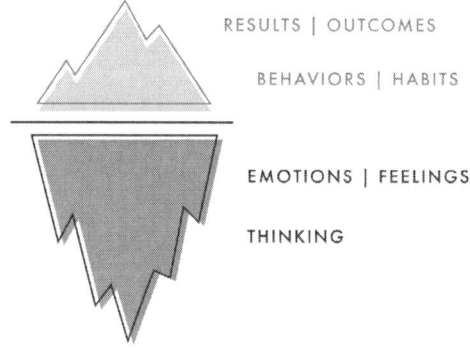

RESULTS | OUTCOMES

BEHAVIORS | HABITS

EMOTIONS | FEELINGS

THINKING

What we achieve is driven by how we think and feel.

particularly helpful in understanding our reactions to stress. In many instances, we simply react to any situation that we perceive as a threat. Often, we allow our stress response to go unchecked. But that doesn't have to be the case, particularly when it comes to chronic stress. When we find ourselves in situations where stress is ongoing and prolonged, we have the opportunity to explore our thoughts, feelings, and reactions rather than simply allow a knee-jerk response. And this is what allows us to change our behaviors, promote resilience, and effectively manage our stress.

When we change the way we perceive a situation, we invite the chance for us to see circumstances as non-threatening instead of threatening. In doing so, we inherently change our brain's neurochemistry and processing, which leads to positive neuroplasticity changes. Thus, as we rewire our brains to better evaluate situations, we naturally enhance our resilience to stress. We allow ourselves to approach choices more rationally and less emotionally. Not only does this reduce the stress we experience in the moment, but it also reduces our tendency to react to other situations in a stressful way in the future.

Ultimately, our goal is to effectively manage stress while building resilience. In the next section, **The Heart Brain**, I will share with you the research-based science of the intelligence of the heart. By better understanding the role of your heart plays in shifting your thinking and emotions, you will be better able to build resilience and regulate your natural stress response. And likewise, this will allow you to better achieve a state of enhanced well-being.

STRESS SUMMARY POINTS

- Stress is a reaction to a real or imagined threat

- Stress enhances our alertness and performance to an extent allowing us to best respond to our environment

- Excessive stress, however, can undermine performance and lead to hyper-alertness

- Excess stress also undermines rational decision-making and promotes emotional, instinctive choices

- Stress induces a "fight-flight-freeze" response triggered by the sympathetic nervous system

- Sensory inputs and perceptions stimulate the amygdala, which perceives the threat and sounds off the alarm

- The hypothalamic-pituitary-adrenal (HPA) axis regulates the autonomic nervous system (sympathetic and parasympathetic nerves) through hormones and nerve stimulation

- The sympathetic nervous system acts like a gas pedal in causing a stress response

- The parasympathetic nervous system acts like a brake in stopping the stress response

- Adrenaline and cortisol are two important compounds involved in the stress response

- Stress can be physical or psychological; acute or chronic

- Both external and internal factors can cause stress

- External factors causing stress may include things like divorce, loss of a loved one, loss of job, etc.

- Internal factors causing stress relate to the thoughts and feelings we have about something

- Chronic stress can cause physical, mental, and emotional symptoms

- Physical manifestations of stress can include headaches, stomach problems, pain, poor sleep and other symptoms

- Mental manifestations of stress can include poor attention, poor concentration, memory difficulty, and disorganized thinking

- Emotional manifestations of stress can include anxiety, depression, and moodiness

- Behavior changes can also indicate stress effects and lead to social isolation, avoidance, and even substance use

- Long-term effects of stress can lead to heart disease, diabetes, infections, cancers, and exhaustion

- Stress effects vary with age, gender, past experiences, and level of development

- Chronic stress can result in a "rewiring" of the brain that perpetuates a stress response and undermines wellness

- Managing stress and wellness can be achieved by engaging positive neuroplasticity processes of the brain

- Redirecting thoughts and reactions associated with stress can enhance positive neuroplasticity effects

The Heart Brain

The heart-brain plays a critical role in building resilience and improving cognitive function.

Follow your heart (brain)

"Educating the mind without educating the heart is no education at all." - Aristotle[57]

INTRODUCTION: ARISTOTLE'S FAVORITE ORGAN

Throughout the ages, many philosophers, scholars, and seculars have recognized the heart as the seat of our soul. In the fourth century B.C., Greek philosopher Aristotle believed the heart was the most important organ of the body. Aristotle described the heart as a three-chambered organ that was the center of vitality as well as the seat of intelligence, movement, and sensation. According to Aristotle, emotions, as well as many of our thoughts, resulted from the way our heart interpreted the sensations we received. These sensations traveled to the heart by way of the blood vessels from other parts of our bodies. This part of Aristotle's philosophy is where we got the term *heartfelt*.[58]

Centuries later, science has now realized that the heart is an intelligent, information-processing organ also. Like our cognitive brains, our heart influences the way we perceive and respond to the world. In 1991, the heart was reclassified as a type of brain by neurocardiologist, Dr. Andrew Armour. Dr. Armour recognized that the heart has its own intrinsic nervous system.[59] In fact, our hearts have over 40,000 nerve cells itself![60] The heart's nervous system produces neuro-transmitters, proteins, and support cells just like our cognitive brain. And our heart brain similarly has the ability to sense internal and external stimuli and to learn and remember.[61]

Our heart has also been reclassified as being a part of our bodies' endocrine or hormonal system. The heart produces several hormones. Some help regulate our body's blood pressure and circulation. These types of hormones include atrial natriuretic factor and brain natriuretic peptide. The heart also secretes hormones that help regulate its own activities as well as how we interact with others.[62] One of these hormones, oxytocin, is commonly referred to as the love or bonding hormone.[63] Thus, as you can see, our hearts share many similar functions with our cognitive brains, which is why it has become designated as a type of brain itself.

HEART TALK: WHAT YOUR HEART BRAIN TELLS YOUR COGNITIVE BRAIN

"When the heart speaks, the mind finds it indecent to object"
- Milan Kundera[64]

Researchers now understand that our heart brain is important in regulating our emotions, building resilience, and improving our clarity of thought. We previously learned that many of our emotions originate in the limbic region of our brains. Likewise, rational thought and our ability to make decisions are linked to our prefrontal cortex. If this is the case, then how does our heart influence these areas? How does our heart affect the way we feel and think?

In reality, our heart brains communicate with our cognitive brains in a number of ways. You might be surprised to learn that the heart sends more information to our brains than our brain sends to our hearts. The signals that our brains receive from the heart affect several cognitive brain areas on a regular basis. Parts of the brain involved in strategic thinking, decision-making, behavior responses, creativity, and even self-regulation all have inputs from the heart.[65] Though our cognitive brain is usually the one to call the shots, our heart brain has plenty to say in the final outcome.

The heart brain communicates with the cognitive brain in a number of ways. Specifically, the heart routinely uses 4 different ways to send messages and signals to our brain. In some instances, our heart brain uses hormones and neurochemicals to communicate information. In other instances, direct nerve inputs are used. The following summarizes these 4 primary ways that our heart brains influence our cognitive brains on a regular basis.[66]

1. NEUROLOGICAL COMMUNICATION[67]

For decades, we have known that the cognitive brain sends nerve signals to the heart. Sympathetic and parasympathetic nerve inputs to the heart regulate a number of functions like heart rate and heart muscle contractions. But the heart also has its own internal nervous system also sends information to the cognitive brain as well. The information that the heart provides to the brain is more extensive than we previously thought. It was once believed that the heart simply gave the brain feedback about heart rate, blood pressure, and other heart functions. But we now know the information provided by the heart goes well beyond this.

Currently, our heart brain uses two neurological pathways to communicate with our cognitive brain. One travels through the spinal cord and one doesn't. But they both connect to the several parts of our brains that include limbic regions and our prefrontal cortex. As a result, our heart brain has the ability to influence how we feel and think based on the type of inputs that it provides. This information is being constantly relayed by our hearts, and therefore, our hearts routinely affect how we feel and think at any given moment.

2. BIOCHEMICAL COMMUNICATION[68]

The heart produces several different types of hormones that communicate with the brain via a biochemical mechanism. For example, atrial natriuretic factor and other hormones provide information to the brain that helps it regulate our bodies' fluids and electrolytes. But these are not the only hormonal communications from the heart. Heart hormones also interact with our immune system, and they can affect our motivations and behaviors. The biochemical influences between the heart and brain appear to be much more involved than previously thought.

As mentioned previously, the heart also produces the hormone oxytocin. In fact, it makes as much of this hormone as the brain itself. When produced by the heart, oxytocin can influence several brain responses. For one, oxytocin encourages social bonding. But likewise, it also affects how tolerant and trusting we are, and it influences the types of thoughts we have. Not only does our heart influence our thoughts, feelings and behaviors through direct nerve inputs to the brain. It also does this through hormonal effects as well.[69]

3. BIOPHYSICAL COMMUNICATION[70]

Each time our heart muscle contracts, the circulation in our bodies is pushed forward to help nourish our body's cells and to help remove cellular waste. But same pulsations also create a pressure wave that has its own energy force. This pressure wave, created by our heart's muscle contractions, is another form of communication between the heart and brain. In fact, the heart uses this more physical way of communicating as a way to reach all the organs in the body.

Biophysical communications of the heart are less well

understood than other forms of heart communications. However, it is believed that pressure waves and the energy signals they provide help synchronize the way the different organs respond. Therefore, these energy pulses may also help coordinate heart and brain functions as a result. Biophysical communications between the heart and brain also include measures like heart rate variability (HRV). This phenomenon will be discussed in greater detail in the subsequent section.

4. ENERGETIC COMMUNICATION[71]

In addition to pulse waves, our heart brains also emit electrical and magnetic energies. The heart's electrical energy has been estimated to be 60 times higher than that of our cognitive brains. Likewise, the heart's magnetic field has been measured at 100 times the strength of the brain, and it projects in all directions. If you combine these estimates, the electromagnetic field of a person's heart is roughly 5,000 times greater than their cognitive brain, and its effects can potentially be encountered as far as 6 feet away!

Within our brains, information is often communicated through the use of patterns. This has specific relevance to the way our hearts use electromagnetic fields. As the heart's patterns of electrical and magnetic energies change, so does the information that it provides. In other words, by changing its energy patterns, our heart is able to provide our cognitive brains with different information inputs. This is yet another way that our hearts likely influences how we feel and think.

"Positive emotions are the building blocks of resilience, physical health, everyday effectiveness, and fulfilling relationships. We need moments of positivity." - **Barbara Fredrickson, PHD University Chapel Hill, Author of Positivity**[72]

MEASURING RESILIENCE WITH HEART RATE VARIABILITY (HRV)

The first written description of the heart's rate and rhythm appeared in ancient Greek texts. Herophilus, a Greek physician and scientist, was the first to measure heart rate by taking a person's pulse. In the 1700s, researcher Stephen Hales later noted that the heart's beat was inherently irregular in nature. However, he also noted that this irregularity formed predictable patterns over time.[73] A century later, others then discovered that these irregularities were affected by our breathing. All of this provided key developments in our current understanding of heart rates and rhythms, and it also led to insights we gained about heart rate variability.[74]

The normal beat-to-beat variability in your heart rate is known as heart rate variability, or HRV for short. Though it may seem like your heart rate is constant and monotonous, it actually isn't. The microseconds between every heart beat changes ever so slightly, resulting in constant irregularity. You might think that these heart irregularities are unhealthy, but this is not necessarily the case. In fact, higher levels of HRV tend to suggest a stronger ability to adapt to change and tends to boost our overall health.[75]

So, exactly why is HRV important? In short, HRV provides a direct measurement of the health of our autonomic nervous system. Our autonomic nervous system is the one that tends to run on autopilot. It is comprised of our sympathetic nervous system, which is part of our fight, flight, and freeze response. It also involves our parasympathetic nervous system, which tends to slow things down. The constant interaction between our sympathetic and parasympathetic systems is what accounts for these subtle variations in our heart rate.

Research now links HRV to various health outcomes. For example, a low HRV tends to imply that our autonomic nervous system is less robust than it should be. This means we are less prepared to react to changes in our environment. This occurs naturally with aging, but it also occurs with chronic health conditions as well. At the same time, an erratic and irregular HRV suggests we are off balance. In this instance, our sympathetic and parasympathetic systems are out of sync. This is also less than ideal in terms of our health.[76]

An ideal HRV is one that demonstrates a normal degree of variability. It is one whose pattern is more predictable and less erratic. A healthy HRV suggests that you have a balanced and healthy interplay between your sympathetic and parasympathetic systems. When this occurs, you are better equipped to adapt to change, and you are more resilient and flexible in your responses. When you enjoy a healthy HRV, you increase your capacity to make wiser decisions, choose more appropriate behaviors, and in turn, enjoy better health. In other words, a healthy HRV suggests your heart brain is able to function at its very best.[77]

Consider a tennis player who is waiting for her opponent to serve the tennis ball. As she waits, she must be in an active state of anticipation. If she is flat-footed and standing still, she will be slower to react to the serve. If she is already moving in one direction or another, she may be out of position. But if she balances herself well between action and inaction, she will be best prepared for what's about to happen. This is similar to the way our autonomic nervous system functions. When our sympathetic and parasympathetic systems are well balanced, we can function at our best. And when this balance exists, we tend to exhibit a healthy and predictable HRV pattern.

Our goal is to choose behaviors that promote a healthy HRV rather than one that is constantly too low or too erratic. A healthy HRV is one that demonstrates a smoother and more predictable pattern of variation between heart beats. This pattern of HRV is associated with optimal health and wellness. Likewise, a healthy HRV indicates our heart brain is performing well. While negative emotions and stress tend to undermine our ability to achieve a healthy HRV, positive emotions do just the opposite. And this plays a notable role in helping us obtain a healthy HRV and state of coherence.

ACHIEVING AND BENEFITTING FROM COHERENCE

When we are able to achieve a healthy HRV, we are said to be in a state of psychological and physical coherence. In other words, a harmony exists among our thoughts, body, and emotions that lets us function at our very best. When we enjoy coherence, our HRV takes on a smooth, sine-wave pattern. In other words, the variations between each heart beat is predictable and more consistent. In contrast, when a state of harmony is lacking, and we are not in coherence, our HRV is more erratic and less predictable. Thus, by examining our HRV, we can immediately know whether or not we are enjoying a state of coherence or not.[78]

At first glance, it may seem like coherence is simply a state of relaxation. But in actuality, these two states are quite different. Coherence indicates a well-balanced state regardless of whether you are relaxed or active. When we are relaxed, we tend to have a slower heart rate. When we become active, our heart rate naturally accelerates. But in both instances, we may be in a state of either low or high coherence. We might be extremely relaxed with a low heart rate but have a highly erratic HRV (incoherence). Likewise, we may be quite active with a higher heart rate but enjoy a highly predictable and smooth HRV (coherence). This is an important distinction.[79]

Coherence represents a balanced and energized state where our sympathetic and parasympathetic systems are well synchronized. When this occurs, we are at our best to deal with any changes that come our way. Our heart rate may be fast or slow, depending on the level of activity we are performing. But the variability between our heart beats is predictable and indicates balance. A synchronized, coherent state thus allows us to function at a high level of efficiency, and it is characterized by strong emotional stability and mental clarity.[80] When coherence is present, our heart, brain, and body are well-aligned and ready to respond in the best way possible.

How do we achieve coherence? Research shows that the emotions we feel have a tremendous effect on heart rate variability and coherence. Negative feelings like anger, frustration, anxiety and stress increase our HRV, and they do so in a very imbalanced way. As a result, our HRV becomes unpredictable, erratic, and out of sync. In contrast, positive feelings do just the opposite. Feelings of appreciation, thankfulness, happiness, and love increase our HRV, and they do so in a balanced manner. Through positive feelings, we therefore improve our capacity to achieve a state of coherence.[81]

It's important to appreciate the difference between emotions and feelings. Emotions are subconscious reactions within our cognitive brain. Our brain reacts to various inputs and generates emotions at a subconscious level. Feelings, on the other hand, represent the conscious way we experience and interpret these emotions. While each of us may experience the same emotion in a specific situation, the feelings we have may be quite different. In other words, we have the ability to consciously choose how to respond to these emotions in a positive or negative way.

Of course, in order for us to take advantage of this opportunity, we must first recognize the emotions we are experiencing. Emotions serve a purpose and are neither positive or negative. For example, emotions of anger may alert you to some injustice or danger. You may experience anger when something happens against your values. However, how you respond to this anger, determines your feelings. When anger appears, you can choose to embrace negative feelings or positive ones. The former is more likely to promote a state of incoherence while the latter does just the opposite.

Positive and negative feelings have the power to encourage/renew or discourage/deplete a state of coherence. I can provide a perfect example of how this affects us each day. Not long ago, my family and I were traveling to California. In anticipation of our trip, I became excited to see my relatives (renewing feeling), yet I was worried we might miss our early-morning flight (depleting feeling). When we arrived to the airport gate on time, I was relieved (renewing). However, I again felt anxious after learning our flight was delayed, which might cause us to miss our connection (depleting). Fortunately, our plane was not delayed for long, and I was able to relax (renewing). But this was once again short-lived after I received a call for our pet sitter who had lost the key to our home (depleting).

In the end, all was fine. But by analyzing my emotional

reactions, I realized the tremendous rollercoaster we often experience through the course of everyday life! While different circumstances triggered different emotions, I had the choice each time to react with positive feelings or negative ones. I could either choose to promote coherence or undermine it. It wasn't that my emotions were inappropriate to the information I received. But my reactions to these emotions determined whether or not I was able to achieve greater or lesser amounts of coherence. If we want to attain a state a coherence, and promote a healthy heart brain, we have to appreciate the impact positive and negative feelings have.

HEARTMATH TECHNIQUES FOR ACHIEVING COHERENCE

HeartMath Institute is an innovative, nonprofit organization that has performed extensive research related to the heart's capacity for intelligence and its effect on coherence. They have developed specific techniques that help relieve stress and empower people to build resilience. This is achieved by bringing physical, mental, and emotional systems into a well-balanced state. In fact, these techniques have been used by the military, healthcare workers, first responders, educators, and high-performance athletes with incredible success. And with over 300 research studies examining their process, it's clear their methods are effective in promoting coherence.[82]

Overall, two important HeartMath techniques are used to help you attain greater coherence. One involves intentionally creating a positive emotional state. By embracing positive feelings that are renewing in nature rather than depleting, you cultivate coherence. This requires conscious awareness of your emotions at any given moment as well as a commitment to respond in a positive way. When you choose to respond in a positive way, your ability to obtain a healthy HRV and a state of coherence naturally follows.[83]

Knowing the emotions that you are experiencing can sometimes be challenging. Because of this, it may be helpful to monitor your HRV. When your HRV is more erratic and unpredictable, you are likely experiencing some type of depleting emotion that has been generated by thought. HeartMath offers tools to track your HRV that can provide such feedback. With the proper feedback, you become better able to recognize when incoherence is present. This information can then encourage you to explore your emotional state more deeply and better appreciate when incoherence may be present.

One of the tools HeartMath offers is its Inner Balance device, which allows you to monitor your HRV on an ongoing basis. I wore one while attending a HeartMath training session and found it to be incredibly revealing. At the beginning of the session, I was feeling happy and enthusiastic to be learning about the heart brain. As a result, my HRV showed a strong state of coherence. But during the course, I noticed that I slipped into incoherence based on my HRV readings. As it turned out, I was allowing a sense of fear to come over me as I questioned my ability to teach heart brain concepts to others. This had caused me to intermittently move from a state of coherence to incoherence.

HeartMath monitoring tools allow us to better appreciate how we react to various situations and circumstances. They enhance our awareness of the thoughts and feelings we are experiencing. This allows us to better understand how we are reacting, and it also shows us how we might change our responses. By recognizing thoughts and feelings that are depleting, we can choose to adopt different ones that are renewing. And by embracing greater positivity, we invite greater coherence on a regular basis.

In addition to positivity, you can also use breathing strategies to help promote a state of coherence. Breathing is known to help regulate heart rhythms. In meditation, breathing exercises are used as a relaxation technique to slow the heart rate and focus the mind. However, a different breathing approach can also be used to facilitate coherence.[85] This technique can be used anytime throughout the day, and it is extremely simple and effective. And it is proven to be an effective way to help regain a state of coherence quickly.

The overall technique is quite simple. First, it is important that you pre-visualize a specific place or person that invites extremely positive feelings. This may be a tranquil place you visited on vacation, or it may be a special person in your life. In fact, I encourage people to have a handful of these pre-visualizations on hand. By having a small library of positive memories available, you can tap into these quickly without having to think about it.

With your pre-visualizations in mind, you then focus on your breathing. You begin by taking slow, deep breaths while counting to 4 during both inhalation and exhalation. The pace of your breathing should be relaxed and comfortable. Then, become consciously aware of your heart space as you breathe while recalling your positive pre-visualized memory. Perform this for a single minute at first, and then build to 2 minutes with repeated practice. Amazingly, this is all it takes to help you regain a sense of coherence.

The effect of these simply breathing exercises builds in time. After all, the heart brain has the ability to learn just like our cognitive brain. Thus, if you perform these exercises several times a day, you will find that these will have an additive effect over the ensuing weeks. Not only will you be able to obtain coherence more quickly and with less effort, but the habit will become more engrained into your daily routine. And the longer you practice these techniques, the more persistent your state of coherence becomes.

The wonderful thing about these breathing techniques are their brevity and flexibility as well as their powerful effects. You may choose to do them while waiting in line, at a stop light, or on a phone call. I often perform them while in a conversation and listening to someone else. I find they help improve my attention and be more connected with what is being said. In short, you can use these techniques anytime throughout your day, and you should strive to do them often. You will be amazed at the profound effect this can have on your life.

The reason these techniques work is because they are able to change your brain's chemistries in both the short-term and over time. By improving your HRV and attaining a state of coherence, you enable your heart brain to favorably influence your cognitive brain. This is achieved through all 4 of the communication forms previously mentioned. I have shared these strategies with countless individuals, and all have experienced the incredible benefits they offer. In fact, my husband, a seasoned commercial pilot, teaches it to his flight crew, and our son and his friends use these techniques to better adapt to stress at school. Your heart brain is more powerful than you might have thought.

THE POWER OF YOUR HEART BRAIN

Feelings of appreciation and gratitude produce "feel good" effects throughout all bodily systems. When positivity is practiced, regenerative hormones and neurochemicals are produced. These include substances like endorphins, oxytocin, dopamine, serotonin, and others. These substances play a role in helping maintain wellness, and they also strengthen our immune system. Therefore, it's perfectly understandable how our heart brains can help regulate all of our bodily systems and improve our physical and cognitive wellbeing.

By utilizing HeartMath techniques, and by recognizing our emotions and reactions, we can approach each and every day in a more positive manner. I have witnessed the power of my heart brain in action, and so have many others. The following is a testimonial of one such example of a client who shared the powerful impact that her heart brain provided on one particularly stressful day.

Yesterday, I walked into our bathroom and noticed water seeping out from the wall. Apparently, a pipe was leaking from the shower (the only shower we have in our house). I turned off the water and patiently waited for my smart, capable husband to get home and figure out a fix (or determine if we needed to start gathering our pennies).

The "old me" would have spiraled out of control. I would have been irritated, frustrated, angry, and stressed out. The mishap would have ruined my day and perhaps my entire weekend. And in all likelihood, it would have probably ruined everyone else's weekend who had to be around me. I would have probably spent most of my day searching for homes online, swearing to somehow never live in a house with problems again. In other words, I would have let my emotions get the better of me.

Don't get me wrong. I wasn't thrilled with the catastrophe I had encountered. But the "new" me, the one that has learned to respond instead of react, showed up that day. I decided I wasn't going to let my unexpected circumstances determine my attitude. Instead, I used the HeartMath techniques to change my perspective and choose to be positive instead of negative. The shift was not only tangible but immediate.

I rolled out my yoga mat, and my son picked out a record (The Doors!). We then proceeded to do a yoga flow session and spent the rest of the day offline enjoying quality time together. It was a truly fulfilling day. The HeartMath techniques offer benefits well beyond self-awareness. You can be self-aware and still know being an impatient bitch while letting stress wreak havoc on your insides. But by combining self-awareness with positivity, HeartMath can not only change your perspective but your entire physiology. THAT'S where the real magic is!

Scientists and researchers are just beginning to understand the power that our heart brain has in relation to our overall health. Many once believed the nervous system in the heart was only involved in regulating how fast and strong the heart muscle worked. But this is no longer the case. The heart's nervous system is intimately connected to our cognitive brain, and it communicates extensively with all body systems through a variety of ways. Thus, by all accounts, the heart truly is a brain of its own. Failing to appreciate this can cause us to miss incredible opportunities for holistic wellness.

Without question, the environments that we experience today are certainly complicated. Commuter traffic, social media overload, financial pressures, and of course, pandemics pose challenges that we must face. Though they may be different from the threats of lions, tigers and bears, they remain real threats. Therefore, we must find ways to effectively deal with these stresses in healthy ways. Using your heart to cultivate coherence is part of this recipe. In doing so, you can better align your head with your heart and enjoy the benefits this congruence brings.

Our heart, as a brain, has the ability to learn. Just like exercising to build muscle and endurance, the more frequently you use HeartMath techniques, the stronger your heart brain will become. This will not only build greater levels of resilience but likewise create healthier habits in how you respond to stress. By tapping into the power of your heart, you promote wellness of your cognitive brain as well as your entire body. And this includes your enteric nervous system, which is also known as your **Gut Brain.**

HEART BRAIN SUMMARY POINTS

- In 1991 the heart was designated a brain by Dr. Andrew Armour, a Neurocardiologist

- The heart has its own nervous system, like the brain, consisting of more than 40,000 neurons

- The heart is also an endocrine organ and produces hormones that have remote effects

- Our heart brain communicates with our cognitive brain in four specific ways, which includes neurological, biochemical, biophysical, and energetic messaging

- Neurological communication travels via the vagus nerve and other nerve pathways to the medulla, limbic system, and cortex. The primary effects are through the autonomic nervous system, which includes sympathetic and parasympathetic pathways

- Biochemical communication occurs through hormones produced by the heart, which includes oxytocin, atrial natriuretic factor, and other substances

- Biophysical communication occurs through mechanical pulsations generated from the heart pumping and pulses waves traveling through the circulation

- Energetic communication occurs through electromagnetic fields generated by the heart

- Neurological communications affect emotions, thoughts, and behaviors through both limbic and cortical influences

- Biochemical communications have been shown to influence motivation, behavior, and immune function

- Biophysical communications promote synchronizing effects in all body organ systems, which includes heart rate variability (HRV)

- Energetic communications exert effects through an electromagnetic field that is 5,000 times stronger than the cognitive brain and can be perceived 6 feet away

- The signals that the heart sends to the brain affect brain centers involved in strategic thinking, decision-making, reaction times, creativity and self-regulation.

- The heart brain plays an important role in our emotional experience. The experience of an emotion results from the brain, heart, and body acting in concert.

- HRV describes the beat-to-beat variability that normally occurs in our heart rate

- HRV is linked to health based on its level of synchrony and frequency

- Low HRV is associated with aging and some diseases

- Erratic, poorly synchronized HRV occurs with stress and negative feelings

- Synchronized HRV at higher levels are linked to optimized health and wellness

- Coherence is a state where the mind, body, and emotions are in harmony and well-balanced

- The heart brain can be used to achieve coherence, and HRV can be used to monitor its achievement

- Coherence is not the same as relaxation. Both increase parasympathetic activity, but relaxation is a low energy state while coherence is a high energy state

- Coherence provides a sense of calm, enhanced mental clarity, and increased resilience

- Renewing (positive) emotions such as appreciation create a more ordered, harmonious pattern reflecting that the activity between the sympathetic and parasympathetic systems is synchronized

- Depleting (negative) emotions such as anger, frustration, impatience or anxiety create an irregular, chaotic HRV pattern, indicating that the activity between the sympathetic and parasympathetic systems is not in synchrony

- HeartMath techniques can be used to attain coherence by intentionally adopting positive feelings and thoughts

- HeartMath breathing techniques can also be used to quickly achieve coherence while simultaneously adopting positivity

- The power of our heart brain remains underappreciated, but it has profound effects in generating total health and wellness through its ability to promote coherence among all bodily systems

The Gut Brain

The gut-brain connection has a significant impact on your cognitive vitality, overall health, and emotional wellbeing.

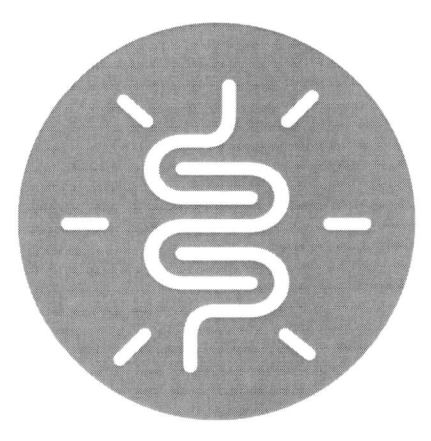

Trust your gut (brain)

"Gut feelings are guardian angels.
Listen to them." - Unknown

INTRODUCTION: MORE THAN JUST A GUT FEELING

Your gut brain, formally referred to as your enteric nervous system, has more intuitive intelligence than you probably imagine. Have you ever had a "gut feeling" about something? Your gut instincts may have warned you that something wasn't right. Or it may have encouraged you to take action. Though different from our other brains, your gut brain still plays an important role. In fact, science has shown that listening to your gut feelings is a good idea!

The gastrointestinal system is a much more complex system than most people realize. Of course, its primary function is to digest, absorb, and transport the foods we eat. But in addition, it has many other important functions. Our gut has an extensive sensory system, and it contains the vast majority of our body's immune system. Likewise, our gut communicates with the other organs of our body through a complex signaling system. As a result, this makes our gut especially important in managing our overall health and wellness.

For more than a century, scientists have investigated the various roles our guts play in maintaining health. As far back as the early 19th century, researchers believed that our gut had the capacity for both intelligence and feelings. More recently, Dr. Michael Gershon has described our gut as being more adept in these areas than our heart. These perspectives led him to refer to the gut as our "second brain." In fact, this served as the title of several of his publications.[86]

While I agree that our gut is capable of intelligence and emotion, it doesn't have a greater capacity for these functions than our heart brain. After all, our heart brain is able to regulate our thinking and feelings while also regulating many gastrointestinal functions. This is not to minimize the role that our gut brain plays in our wellbeing. However, it does imply that it's a combination of all of our brains (head, heart, and gut) that offers us the ability to attain deeper understanding and insights. In other words, our gut brain is on equal footing with our other sources of intelligence.

THE GUT'S COMMUNICATION SYSTEM

You might say the gut has a mind of its own. Our gastrointestinal system is the largest sensory organ in the body and is completely capable of functioning on its own. On average, most adults' gastrointestinal tract is about 20 feet in length. Based on this, scientists estimate its inner surface area is about the same size as a studio apartment! In addition, the gut's own nervous system contains over 500 million nerve cells that are able to communicate with one another forming a vast network of connections.[87]

An array of neurochemicals and hormones allow nerve cells to pass along important messages to one another. As different events and experiences occur, substances are produced and released that allow nerve cell communications. Communication is important for any extensive network of nerve cells, but it's also beneficial in another way. Such a system gives our gut brain the capacity to learn and store memories. And it also provides the means by which our gut brain influences the way we think and feel.

Many of the neurochemicals used by our gut brains are neurotransmitters, and most are the same ones found in our central nervous system. These include substances like dopamine, serotonin, norepinephrine (adrenaline) and GABA. This means that our gut brains not only produce these neurotransmitters but also have nerve cell receptors for them as well. Because of this, our gut brain is able to communicate with our head brain quite well. This is how our gut brain and head brain are able to influence one another in a reciprocal fashion.

While scientists are still discovering the many functions

of these neurotransmitters, some have been identified. For example, GABA has positive effects on our mood, relieves pain, and reduces fear responses. It also helps burn fats and regulates blood pressure. Dopamine, which is in large amounts in our gut, affects decision-making, memory, and motivation. And serotonin, known to affect mood and memory, also plays a role in regulating gastrointestinal motility, appetite, and digestion. In fact, over 90 percent of the body's serotonin can be found in our gut.[88]

THE GUT-BRAIN CONNECTION

Several researchers have recognized that a connection exists between our gut and our brain. Dr. Emeran Mayer has labelled this as the mind-gut connection and suggests both organs communicate through a unique biochemical language. He refers to this language as a form of microbe-speak.[89] This connection between the gut and brain allows both systems to play a part in guiding our emotions and thoughts. Likewise, it would also explain why we might rely on gut instincts and gut feelings when faced with a difficult choice.

Neuroscientist Antonio Damasion notes that body sensations, or somatic markers, frequently reflect specific emotions. For example, a rapid heartbeat can indicate anxiety or stress, or nausea may reflect disgust. According to his somatic marker hypothesis, these sensations in the body influence the decisions we make. In fact, evidence now suggests that these somatic markers are processed in the ventromedial prefrontal cortex (VMPFC) and the amygdala of the brain. In this way, they could play an important role in decision-making.[90]

For a long time, it was not well appreciated the effect our gut has on our mental and emotional states. But increasingly, research indicates that gut neurons, termed viscerofugal neurons, relay information all the way from our gut lining to various regions of our spinal cord and brain.[91] Through neurochemicals and neurotransmitters, these gut neurons influence several regions of our central nervous center. This includes areas like our limbic system, amygdala, hippocampus, and prefrontal cortex. Thus, it's not surprising that these inputs can affect how we feel, our level of motivation, our self-awareness, and our thoughts.[92]

Naturally, the communications between the gut and brain are bidirectional. Not only does our brains send signals to our gut, but our gut also sends messages to our brains. In this regard, it is now estimated that 90 percent of the information communicated originates in the gut itself.[93] That's a pretty impressive figure! With this degree of influence, it's easy to appreciate the impact our gut brain can have on our perceptions, feelings, and choices.

YOUR MICROBIOME'S IMPACT ON BRAIN FUNCTION

To understand how our gut brain generates this large volume of information, it's important to appreciate the role our microbiome plays. Our microbiome is the collection of bacteria, viruses, fungi and other microorganisms that line our gastrointestinal tract. Unlike microorganisms that cause illness, the ones in our microbiome are actually "good" bacteria, viruses, and fungi. They help us digest foods, boost our immune system, and serve a variety of important health functions. And they are also a major source of neurochemicals that relay important pieces of information.

The word microbiome means small colony. But while the microorganisms are tiny, their numbers are not. In fact, trillions of these microorganisms exist in each of our guts. The number of genes in all the microbes in a single person's microbiome is 200 times the number in the human genome.[94] Therefore, it's not surprising that the substances released from our microbiome serve as an important source of information. In many cases, the neurochemicals released by our microbiome result in local changes within our gut. But they also account for a large number of signals sent to our brains.

Just like your fingerprint or genetic makeup, you have a microbiome that's unique to you. Your gut began to colonize with microbes right after you were born. As you passed through the birth canal, you collected some of these microbes. Then, as you encountered different environments and ate various foods, your microbiome continued to evolve. In fact, science has shown that our microbiome is constantly changing. We can actually change our microbiome by changing our diets, and this can result in favorable or unfavorable effects.[95] This is yet another reason why healthy dietary choices are so important to our well-being.

The microbes in our microbiome receive most of the nutrients from the foods we eat. Changes in our diet can allow some microbes to thrive while being detrimental to others. In this way, diet can influence the composition of your microbiome, and in turn, affect how your brain performs as well. Many have recognized that mood swings or brain fog can actually result from an unhealthy microbiome. Though science is in its infancy in this area, significant evidence already supports these connections.

From a personal perspective, I have had such experiences. For many years, I have suffered from digestive issues and food allergies. I suspected that the many antibiotics I had taken as a teen for acne may have negatively affected my microbiome. But despite eating a balanced diet of natural, organic foods, my problems persisted. I then consulted with a gastroenterologist who guided me in how to reestablish a diverse and healthy microbiome. Within days, my digestive problems had improved significantly. And most interestingly, my mood improved as did my clarity of thought.

While diet is a major factor in the microbiome you have, it's not the only one. Where you live, environmental exposures, personal contacts, and medications also influence the types of microbes in your gut. Likewise, stress also plays a major role in the health of your microbiome. A number of strategies may therefore be used to enjoy a healthier microbiome. In doing so, we not only improve our digestive health but our capacity for wellness throughout the body and mind.

STRESS AND THE GUT

As we discussed previously stress levels have significant influence on our wellbeing. Affecting our brain, heart and gut ability to function at their best, stress may well be the biggest overall threat to these three centers of intelligence. Stress can egatively impact many systems, often affecting the immune system the most. Given that over 70 percent of our immune cells reside in our gut, it's not surprising that stress influences our gastrointestinal health.

Our bodies react to acute stress in a rather predictable way. Our heart beats faster, our pupils dilate, and we become hyperalert. But at the same time, our digestive system shuts down. Cortisol and other stress hormones promote our circulation to preferentially flow to our brain and muscles. But it reduces blood flow to our gastrointestinal system. In this instance, these shifts triggered by stress makes sense. After all, if a tiger is chasing you, you probably aren't going to be casually eating your lunch! While acute stress responses are important, chronic stress can become a problem for the gut. Chronic stress triggers inflammation of our intestinal lining, and over time, this leads to weakening of the intestinal barrier. Gut bacteria can then enter into the body and cause a variety of health problems. This includes gastrointestinal problems that result in bloating, indigestion, heartburn, and nausea. And most importantly, chronic stress can exhaust the gut's immune system that can increase the risk of illness even further.

Stress is mediated throughout the body by way of the autonomic nervous system. The autonomic nervous system regulates several involuntary responses like breathing, heart rate, and even digestion. It achieves this through both sympathetic and parasympathetic nerve responses. In essence, our sympathetic nervous system tends to speed things up (think of a gas pedal in your car). In contrast, our parasympathetic nervous system slows things down (like your car's brake). When it comes to chronic stress affecting our gut, it's the parasympathetic effects that are most important.

THE GUT-TO-BRAIN SUPERHIGHWAY

The vagus nerve, which means "wandering" in Latin, is the longest nerve in your body. In fact, it travels all the way from your brainstem to your buttocks. Through its course, the vagus nerve also comes into contact with every organ in your body with the exception of your adrenal gland. Technically your vagus nerve could be considered two nerves, one on the left and right sides of your body. But from a practical perspective, both function together and play an important role in the gut-brain connection.

The vagus nerve influences the body and brain in a variety of ways. It has been described as the "queen of parasympathetic nervous system" as well as the body's "information superhighway." Its bidirectional flow of information between your internal organs and your brain justify these descriptions. Not only is your vagus nerve involved in regulating your digestive system, heart rate, and breathing, it also regulates your immune response and even your emotions. By relaying information to and from your gut brain to your cognitive brain, your vagus nerve serves an extremely important role in your wellbeing.

One of the important functions of the vagus nerve involves your immune response. A healthy vagal nerve response triggers a cholinergic anti-inflammatory response. This helps balance our immune response and keeps it from be overly active.[96] The vagus nerve also innervates your thymus, spleen, and lymph tissue in the gut. As a result, it can directly interact with your immune system to help encourage an immune reaction proportionate to the need.

Your vagus nerve also provides a direct link between your brain and your microbiome. This communication pathway provides real-time information about how well your digestive system is functioning. Similarly, your vagus nerve monitors your breathing and regulates your heart rate. By providing information to your brain about your breathing patterns, your brain then adjusts your heart rate accordingly. This coordinated response is all carried out by the vagus nerve.

As noted previously, chronic stress can undermine wellness in a variety of ways. Therefore, the goal is to either avoid stress as best as possible or reduce its negative effects. One of the best ways to reduce negative stress effects is through building increased vagal tone. When your vagal tone is increased, you enjoy greater resilience and can tolerate stress more effectively. This allows you to return more rapidly to a state of mental, emotional, and physical coherence.

But how do you increase your vagal tone? One of the easiest and best ways to increase your vagal tone is through your breathing, as noted by Dr. Navaz Habib in his book, *Activate Your Vagus Nerve.*[97] In essence, vagal activity is at its best during exhalation. The deeper your exhalation, the more vagal response you will enjoy. Unfortunately, few of us recognize the importance of deep exhalation. But by concentrating on your breathing in this manner, you can easily boost your vagal tone.

Dr. Habib suggests first assessing how functional your breathing currently is. This can be done by placing one hand on your stomach and the other on your chest. Once your hands are in place, take a deep breath and observe whether or not your shoulders move. If so, then you are likely not fully engaging your diaphragm, which indicates a reduced capacity for achieving strong vagal tone. But by making a conscious effort to breathe more effectively using your diaphragm and fully exhaling, this can be easily corrected.[98] And in turn, you will enjoy greater stress resilience and health as a result.

MEASURING STRESS RESILIENCE WITH VAGAL TONE

As mentioned, neurochemicals and hormones account for many communications between our gut and our brain. Our microbiome plays an important role in this communication. But at the same time, our gut and brain communicate via another major pathway. This pathway involves the vagal nerve, which is a major part of our parasympathetic nervous system. In fact, the vagus nerve is responsible for 75 percent of all parasympathetic activity in our body.

While it's difficult to know exact amounts, it is estimated that the vagus nerve accounts for 90 percent of all communications coming from the gut to the brain. Likewise, it also provides inputs from the brain to the gut. Functioning as an information superhighway, vagus nerve activity can influence gut motility, digestion, mood, stress responses, immune signaling as well as microbiome balance. And when functioning well, it serves to promote strong gut health.

People with healthy vagal nerve functioning are described as having "high vagal tone." When someone has high vagal tone, their brain and body is more resilient and can accommodate stress better. They can quickly transition from an excited, sympathetic state to a relaxed, parasympathetic one. For example, someone with high vagal tone would recover more quickly from a heated argument when compared to someone with low vagal tone.

The type of vagal tone we have is directly linked to the amount of chronic stress we experience and are our response to that stress. As stress becomes chronic, we become more likely to experience a state of constant sympathetic nervous system stimulation. Level of cortisol and other neurochemicals like adrenaline become constantly elevated. In response, our parasympathetic nervous system, via the vagus nerve, must attempt to balance this elevated sympathetic state. And over time, it becomes weakened leading to a state of low vagal tone.

People with low vagal tone are more sensitive to stress and at greater risk for disease. They often describe having difficulty controlling their emotions. Likewise, several conditions have been associated with low vagal tone. These include chronic fatigue syndrome, rheumatoid arthritis, and multiple sclerosis. It may also lead to abnormal heart rate, elevated blood pressure, and a variety of digestive complaints. Unable to keep the sympathetic response to stress in check, people with low vagal tone become vulnerable to a variety of problems. And this includes problems involving your gut.

HEARTMATH TECHNIQUES FOR ACHIEVING COHERENCE

Our stress response to a large extent occurs without us knowing it. The autonomic nervous system responds involuntarily to the stress we experience. Despite this, however, we do have the ability to self-regulate the intensity of its response. In other words, we have some degree of voluntary control over our involuntary reactions. Just like we have the ability to adjust how fast and deep we breath, we can also influence our stress response. If done well, this allows us to avoid a low vagal tone state and maintain a higher one.

You can determine your vagal tone by measuring your heart rate variability (HRV). A high HRV indicates you have low vagal tone while a low HRV means the opposite. But in either case, you can enhance your vagal tone through a series of activities that strengthen and promote a parasympathetic state. Performing these activities on a regular basis will serve to increase your vagal tone and level of resilience.[99] In short, this is referred to as vagal toning.

In the previous chapter on the heart brain, HeartMath techniques were described in detail. These approaches enhance vagal tone through breathing exercises, focusing on the heart, and recreating positive experiences and emotions.[100] Through these techniques, we stimulate our parasympathetic nervous system, which increases vagal tone. This results in a more relaxed state of being while improving digestion. Similarly, it also leads to higher amounts of GABA and serotonin that are helpful in reducing chronic stress effects.

Other techniques may also be used for vagal toning. For example, deep diaphragmatic breathing can be used to stimulate the vagus nerve and enhance parasympathetic responses. This is accomplished with a gradual, deep inhalation over 4 seconds, following by holding the breath for 7 seconds, and finally, a gradual exhalation over 8 seconds (The 4-7-8 Method). The exhalation stimulates the parasympathetic response and increases vagal tone. This technique is particularly useful when experiencing situations with high levels of performance anxiety.[101]

Other activities also stimulate the parasympathetic nervous system and vagal tone. Gargling, laughing, singing and humming can enhance vagal tone because the vagus nerve is connected to our vocal cords and throat muscles. Vibration and sound have also been used in this regard. Similarly, exercise, yoga, and even hugging increases one's parasympathetic state.[102] For me personally, I use yoga, regular exercise and the HeartMath techniques as part of my vagal toning routine. But I also use crystal singing bowls intermittently. I like this technique because it has a positive effect on brainwaves, heart rhythm and vagal tone simultaneously.

Through these types of vagal toning activities, we can strengthen our level of stress resilience over time. By committing to this on a regular basis, we allow new brain pathways to develop that enable us to better control our stress response. As previously mentioned, this has powerful benefits on our cognitive brain and heart brain. And it also has tremendous benefits for our gut brain as well.

THE POWER OF YOUR GUT BRAIN

Recent scientific revelations are showing the fascinating potential our gut brains have on the human experience. New technologies have deepened our understanding of this potential, yet at the same time, this field of study remains in its early stages. Some of the best resources on these subjects currently include works written by Giulia Enders[103], Dr. Emeran Mayer[104], and Scott Anderson[105]. These can help you further explore what is and isn't known about our gut brain, and where future research is moving.

Through my own research into this subject, I have gained tremendous insights into my own health and wellbeing. On many occasions, I found myself vomiting as a child for no apparent reason at the time. I was otherwise healthy, and these episodes weren't related to any specific food poisoning and other illness. I have since realized these were simply gut-related reactions to various situations and stresses that I faced. In other words, my gut brain reacted without me having a conscious awareness of the stress I was experiencing.

Some of my childhood years were filled with tremendous uncertainty. We moved three times during the year that I finished second grade and entered into the third. My parents separated, reunited, and then divorced during this time as well. And after that year, we then moved yet again. Being that young, I had lacked the vocabulary to express my feelings well, but my gut spoke for me. Deep down, my gut let me know I wasn't handling things very well.

All of us have experienced gut feelings about something from time to time. Without any facts or data to back things up, something tells us things aren't right. This is often referred to as a gut feeling or gut instinct, which is more accurate than most imagine. Interestingly, I have found these to be quite reliable on many occasions. They have guided me in the right direction when I had little to no information about a situation. Over time, I have come to trust these instincts.

Listening to your gut brain is quite important. For me, my gut increases my awareness of my unconscious feelings. If my gut feels uncomfortable or tense, I know I need to stop and self-reflect. Nearly every time when this happens, I find there is some concern, fear, or worry that I have not acknowledged or addressed. By identifying these feelings, I can them explore my thoughts and experiences that might be fueling them. Ultimately, this makes me more aware and informed, which allows me to make better choices. And I have my gut brain to thank for that.

Learning to trust your gut is difficult and requires courage. Blindly trusting in a gut instinct is naturally scary because it isn't clearly supported by logical explanations. But by integrating these insights from your gut brain with those of your heart brain and cognitive brain, you can gain much deeper insights about any situation. Not only will this allow you to make better choices in life, but it will also help you discover your true, authentic self.

GUT BRAIN SUMMARY POINTS

- The Gut Brain is formally referred to as the Enteric Nervous System (ENS)

- Our gut has over 500 million neurons and is over 20 feet in length

- The Gut Brain has an extensive nervous system and communication network

- One component of this communication network involves neurochemicals, neurotransmitters, and hormones

- Neurotransmitters known to be present in the Gut Brain include dopamine, GABA, serotonin, and norepinephrine among others

- Roughly 90% of the body's serotonin and 50% of the body's dopamine is found in the gut

- There is a dialogue between head and gut via the Gut Brain Axis that is bidirectional with 90% of the communications coming from the gut to the brain

- The biochemical component of this communication has been termed microbe-speak by some scientists

- Somatic Marker Hypothesis describes how bodily sensations are associated with emotions, and these sensations (including those in the gut) can guide decision-making

- Our microbiome is a community of trillions of different microbes that line our gastrointestinal tract

- Our microbiome helps with digestion, immune function, and a variety of other health-related activities

- Our microbiome also plays a role in gut-brain communications by producing and releasing neurochemicals and hormones

- Our microbiome is constantly changing and varies based on our diet, environments, contacts, and medications to which we are exposed

- Stress affects all three brains (cognitive, heart and gut)

- The autonomic nervous system in an involuntary nervous system that responds to stress through sympathetic and parasympathetic responses

- Stress triggers a sympathetic response (fight or flight) that enables us to react to threats

- The parasympathetic system counters the sympathetic system and allows us to recover from stress

- Chronic stress can be detrimental because it creates an imbalance between sympathetic and parasympathetic systems

- Sympathetic responses slow gut functions while parasympathetic restores them

- Chronic stress and excessive sympathetic stimulation lead to inflammation of the gut's lining, weakening of gut barriers, and dysfunction of the gut's immune cells

- Over 70% of our immune cells are located in the gut

- Chronic stress also weakens our parasympathetic system's ability to maintain balance over time

- The vagus nerve accounts for 75% of the body's parasympathetic responses

- The vagus nerve is also another major component of the gut-brain axis and communication system

- The vagus nerve carries 90 percent of all communications from the gut to the brain

- Parasympathetic system health can be defined by high or low levels of vagal tone

- High vagal tone implies good health and a high level of resilience in recovering from stress

- Low vagal tone implies a reduced ability to recover from stress and increases the risk for disease and illness

- High vagal tone promotes good gut brain wellness through stress resilience and better digestive, immune, microbiome, and nerve cell functions

- Vagal tone can be determined by heart rate variability (HRV) with a low HRV suggesting high vagal tone and a high HRV suggesting low vagal tone

- HeartMath exercises represent a great way to achieve higher vagal tone

- Deep diaphragmatic breathing is another technique that may be used in vagal toning (The 4-7-8 Method)

- Yoga, regular exercise, vibrations, sounds, singing, humming and hugging offer additional techniques that promote higher vagal tone

- Use with the knowledge gained from our cognitive brain and heart brain, our gut brain further deepens understanding, improves decision-making, and promotes the authentic self

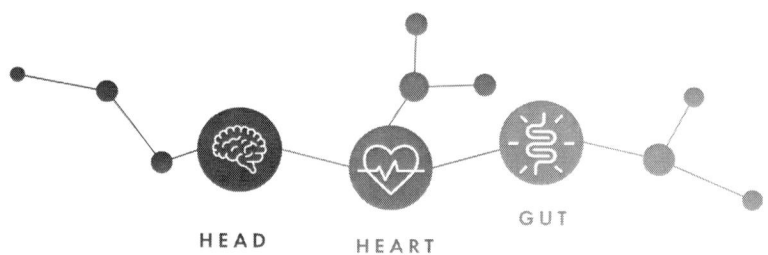

HEAD   HEART   GUT

Conclusion

Connecting the dots for Tri Brain harmony

Your brain, body and gut engage in constant multidirectional communications. While each is labelled as a separate organ, they work in a collaborative and connected way to help us achieve a higher level of consciousness. This higher consciousness is what we call the mind, and it is the culmination of contributions not only from our cognitive brain but from our heart brain and gut brain as well.

THE HEAD

Mindfulness naturally involves our thoughts. Our thoughts help guide our experiences. By understanding how our cognitive brain works, we can better manage the way we think, feel, and behave. By thinking about our thinking, we can become conscious of specific thought patterns and habits that we have. Since non-conscious thoughts often drive our behaviors and feelings, greater awareness of these thoughts can be powerful. With greater awareness, however, we can choose to think differently. In time, these mindfulness practices enable us to develop neuropathways in the brain, which will ultimately lead to healthier thoughts, feelings, and behaviors.

THE HEART

Connecting with our heart allows us to craft a stillness conducive to self-reflection. When we obtain stillness, we engage the intelligence of the heart, which will also improve clarity of thought, feelings and behaviors. While meditation isn't necessarily required to create this stillness, it can help greatly. In this stillness, we use breath and reflection to generate renewing emotions. These include feelings of gratitude, love, and joy that helps engage and regulate our autonomic nervous system. When this happens, we are able to exist in a coherent state of mind and body where we can choose to respond thoughtfully to life's circumstances rather than react. Not only does this allow our heart brain and head brain to connect, but this also promotes greater resilience over time.

THE GUT

The informative and intuitive sense of our gut instincts is yet another source of intelligence. Recognizing that trillions of bacteria in our microbiome are actively involved in reciprocal communication with our head brain is important. This information about our body's environment is extensively provided to the brain via the vagus nerve. As a result, even deeper insights can be gained from our gut brain about our thoughts, feelings, and overall wellbeing. Integrating this information with the intelligence acquired from our head and heart is how intuition is experienced.

TRI BRAIN WELLNESS MODEL

"The intuitive mind is a sacred gift and the rational mind is a faithful servant. We have created a society that honors the servant and has forgotten the gift." – **Albert Einstein**

Before I appreciated how my brain functioned, I allowed it to control me most of the time. But with these insights, I came to appreciate that the brain and the mind are not the same. Certainly, my brain is important, but it is essentially a tool for my mind that allows me the opportunity to experience life and to be creative. My head brain provides a certain type of intelligence that can enhance mindfulness. But like any tool, it must be appreciated for its uses and limitations in order to achieve the best results.

In very much the same way, my heart brain and gut brain are tools to enhance mindfulness and the experiences of life. By integrating these three brains together, each of their intelligences can be used to improve the understanding of self and others as well as life in general. The insights gained through their integration is greater than their sum. And with these insights, it becomes easier to respond to life in a manner that is healthy and constructive rather than simply reacting on a whim.

THE CHOICE IS YOURS

The information that I have shared in this book serves as an entry point to expand your awareness and opportunities for mindfulness. As with many practices, understanding is first required before action can ensure. This book is intended to serve this initial purpose. At this point, you may choose to act on this information or simply consider it for further contemplation. Either way, this represents a choice point for you as the reader. The following, however, offer some comments from others who have decided to pursue a deeper integration of the head, heart and gut brains.

GINA'S COMMENTS:

*"I would love to live like a river flows, carried by the surprise of its own unfolding."~ **John O'Donohue***

This quote provides me with a vision of how I would like to experience life. In reflecting on my life's chapters, I have pursued self-improvement in many ways. I have enjoyed a wonderful 29-year corporate career where I sought extensive professional and executive coaching. Prior to that, I was a competitive athlete and received excellent coaching in swimming. Through these experiences, it became evident that I was more successful if I new the "why" behind the "what."

My first experience with Tri Brain® theory was only a few years ago toward the end of my corporate tenure. Though I have always been committed to the pursuit of wellbeing, the concepts of Tri

Brain® theory completely changed the way I looked at things. When I learned how our head, heart, and gut are interconnected and provide a holistic intelligence, a sudden light bulb went off in my head. By understanding the science behind these three brains, I was able to more fully pursue the level of wellbeing that I wanted.

For me, I think of our three brains as islands. Much of what I know about positive framing originally came from my mother. Positive language, affirmations, and songs became mantras in our home that had become a part of her life after a turbulent and abusive childhood. She used her head brain to guide her thoughts, feelings and behaviors in a positive direction, and it made her one of the most resilient women I have ever known. It would be these same mantras that she remembered right until the end during her battle with Alzheimer's disease. For these reasons, the island of the mind has always been a fascination of mine.

In regards to the heart brain, my closest encounter with this previously was through yoga. As a student of yoga for 20 years, I embraced breathing techniques as a way to ground me and help me stay calm during troubling times. In fact, breathing was how I survived TSA and security checks after 9/11. But I was not aware of the power of our heart brain in offering us a deeper level of intelligence and mindfulness until I encountered Tri Brain® theory. The use of the HeartMath tools has changed my life ever since.

Lastly, the island of the gut brain was something I experienced more personally. For years, I struggled with an array of gut symptoms related to autoimmune conditions, leaky gut syndrome, and hormonal imbalances. I tried every relevant over-the-counter supplement, a number of different diets, and even tried different types of exercises. None of these helped. Eventually, I finally saw an integrative health doctor after I was in my forties. Through a more holistic and interconnected approach, I finally found relief.

Prior to Tri Brain® theory, I essentially treated my head, heart and gut as separate islands. Though temporary reliefs were enjoyed briefly, lasting improvement never arrived. As stress from my corporate job increased, I found myself running on autopilot, reacting to every life circumstance. Anxiety and depression began to develop, and I felt totally disconnected. I was trying to take care of each of the islands best I could, but it wasn't working. That's when I learned about Tri Brain® theory.

Immediately upon working with Tri Brain® theory, I learned to connect these "islands" and treat them as an inter-island, super-highway of information. I learned how the head, heart, and gut brains interconnect, and I became capable of better aligning them in order to improve my overall wellness. These insights taught me the power of choice and the opportunity to choose my responses. They also allowed me to see stress reactions and emotions for what they were and accept them. I have since benefitted from this awareness not only in my career but in all aspects of my life.

These were not the only advantages I have enjoyed using Tri Brain® theory. I have since incorporated heart-centric breathing into my yoga practice and throughout my day. This has allowed me to experience a new level of grounding and centering. I can use these techniques anywhere, anytime to gain greater mindfulness. Tri Brain® theory also taught me to appreciate that gut health is much more than eating the right kind of diet. It too is connected to our head and heart. By treating health holistically, I have been able to mitigate my gastrointestinal problems tremendously.

One of the things I appreciate the most about Tri Brain® theory is that there is science to back up its concepts and practices. We have the power and ability to choose better health and wellness and to realize it. These techniques make us more resilient to handle anything coming our way, and promote healing and growth. I now have the confidence to "live like a river flows," without being afraid. These days, I find myself living more in the present and simply curious about what might be next.

MARYL'S COMMENTS

I have had a lifelong interest in exploring how our brain works. But I thought we only had one which was in our head before encountering Tri Brain® theory. Having attended several workshops, I now appreciate that the collective intelligence we enjoy comes from more that just our head. Our heart and gut play a role as well. Through these teachings, I have gained a much better understanding how each brain works and how they work together.

Perhaps, the most powerful thing I have learned from Tri Brain® theory is how our head brain often reacts to triggers. In situations where we feel threatened, we tend to react emotionally in an effort to protect ourselves. I have noticed that these types of triggers are quite common in my closest relationships. Those we know the best can often push our buttons. Unless we have an awareness about this, we react emotionally rather than rationally. But by exploring the situation in greater detail and/or sharing it with someone else, we can gain insight and improve our relationships.

In addition to these insights, Tri Brain® theory also taught me much about our heart brain. The HeartMath techniques has allowed me to calm my autonomic nervous system. This reduces the level of stress, invites positive happy emotions, and leads to a more love-filled life. I find this particularly helpful in the wee hours of the morning when I am unable to sleep due to specific worries. By using the HeartMath techniques, I am better able to use my heart brain to better control not only my emotions but my thoughts and reactions as well.

Finally, I never had any idea that the nervous system in my gut served as a type of brain. I must admit, I would tend to ignore signals from my gut in the past. It's not that it didn't get my attention, but I just didn't value its input. Now that I am aware of its powerful impact, and its extensive connections with the head and heart brains, I have completely changed my approach.

I now gladly open up to its communications and insights to help me make better choices.

SUMMARY

The most common and immediate insight from those that have experienced Tri Brain® coaching or educational programs is the recognition of moving through life on "auto pilot." As awareness expands, the capability to shift to a higher level of consciousness increases and life experiences take on a new meaning.

BE THE TRANSFORMATIVE CHANGE

"When you change the way you look at things, the things you look at change." **- Unknown**

Our world is ripe for change, and our planet has the potential to be more loving and peaceful if we choose to evolve and better understand ourself and others. We have the power to transform our world by shifting our consciousness, transforming ourselves, and opening our hearts. Tri Brain® theory is a means by which we can accomplish this, and with the insights provided in this book, my hope is that you too will choose to be part of this rewarding experience.

With love,

Elizabeth

References

1.   Wikimedia Commons. "File: Neuronal Synapse.jpg." 2011. Retrieved from https://commons.wikimedia.org/wiki/File:Neuronal_Synapse.jpg

2.   Compound Interest. "A Simple Guide to Neurotransmitters." 2015. Retrieved from https://www.compoundchem.com/2015/07/30/neurotransmitters/

3.   Dispenza, Joe. Breaking the habit of being yourself. Hay House, Inc, 2012.

4.   Mateos-Aparicio, Pedro, and Antonio Rodríguez-Moreno. "The Impact of Studying Brain Plasticity." Frontiers in cellular neuroscience vol. 13 66. 27 Feb. 2019, doi:10.3389/fncel.2019.00066

5.   Ibid.

6.   Doidge, Norman. The brain that changes itself: Stories of personal triumph from the frontiers of brain science. Penguin, 2007.

7.   McKay, Sarah. "These are the 7 habits of highly healthy brains (in order of importance)." YourBrainHealth.com, 2016. Retrieved from http://yourbrain-health.com.au/these-are-the-7-habits-of-highly-healthy-brains-in-order-of-importance/

8.   Ibid.

9.   Ibid.

10.   Ibid.

11.   Ibid.

12.   Goldhill, Olivia. "Scientists say your 'mind' isn't confined to your brain, or even your body." Quartz.com, 2016. Retrieved from https://qz.com/866352/scientists-say-your-mind-isnt-confined-to-your-brain-or-even-your-body/

13.   Salt, William B, M.D. "What is the difference between the mind and the brain?" ShareCare.com, 2019. Retrieved from https://www.sharecare.com/health/teen-perspective-learning-and-memory/what-difference-between-mind-brain

14.   Siegel, Daniel J. Mind: A Journey to the Heart of Being Human (Norton Series on Interpersonal Neurobiology). WW Norton & Company, 2016.

15.   Unilaterality of amygdala

16.   Siegel, Daniel J. Mindsight: The new science of personal transformation. Bantam, 2010.

17.   .Barrett, Lisa Feldman. How emotions are made: The secret life of the brain. Houghton Mifflin Harcourt, 2017.

18. Ibid.

19. Murakami, Hiroki, Ruri Katsunuma, Kentaro Oba, Yuri Terasawa, Yuki Moto-mura, Kazuo Mishima, and Yoshiya Moriguchi. "Neural networks for mindful-ness and emotion suppression." PloS one 10, no. 6 (2015).

20. Ibid.

21. Wolpert, Stuart. "Putting Feelings into Words Produces Therapeutic Effects in the Brain; UCLA Neuroimaging Study Supports Ancient Buddhist Teach-ings." UCLA Newsroom, June 21 (2007): 132-38.

22. Chödrön, Pema. Living beautifully with uncertainty and change. Shambhala Publications, 2012.

23. Krebs, Ruth M., Dorothee Heipertz, Hartmut Schuetze, and Emrah Duzel. "Novelty increases the mesolimbic functional connectivity of the substantia nigra/ventral tegmental area (SN/VTA) during reward anticipation: evidence from high-resolution fMRI." Neuroimage 58, no. 2 (2011): 647-655.

24. Asurian. "Americans Check Their Phones 96 Times a Day." Press Release, 2019. Retrieved from https://www.asurion.com/about/press-releases/amer-icans-check-their-phones-96-times-a-day/

25. Salim, Saima. "How much time do you spend on social media? Research says 142 minutes per day." Digital Information World, 2019. Retrieved from https://www.digitalinformationworld.com/2019/01/how-much-time-do-peo-ple-spend-social-media-infographic.html#

26. Scarpina, Federica, and Sofia Tagini. "The Stroop color and word test." Fron-tiers in psychology 8 (2017): 557.

27. UC Santa Barbara. "Mindfulness." Website, n.d. Retrieved from http://well-ness.sa.ucsb.edu/onlinechallenges/ucsbhappinesschallenge/week-7

28. Ibid.

29. Forbes Quotes. "Thoughts on a business life." Forbes, 2015. Retrieved from https://www.forbes.com/quotes/3539/

30. The American Institute of Stress. "Workplace stress." Website, 2019. Re-trieved from https://www.stress.org/workplace-stress

31. Global Organization for Stress. "Stress facts." Website, n.d. Retrieved from http://www.gostress.com/stress-facts/

32. Hanson, Rick. Hardwiring happiness: The new brain science of contentment, calm, and confidence. Harmony, 2016.

33. Harvard Health. "Understanding the stress response." Website, 2011. Re-trieved from https://www.health.harvard.edu/staying-healthy/understand-ing-the-stress-response

34. Akil, Huda. "How Stress Alters the Brain and Behavior." BrainFacts.org, 2019. Retrieved from https://www.brainfacts.org/neuroscience-in-society/law-economics-and-ethics/2019/how-stress-alters-the-brain-and-behavior-032019

35. Harvard Health, 2011.

36. Ibid.

37. Ibid.

38. Hannibal, Kara E., and Mark D. Bishop. "Chronic stress, cortisol dysfunction, and pain: a psychoneuroendocrine rationale for stress management in pain rehabilitation." Physical therapy 94, no. 12 (2014): 1816-1825.

39. Harvard Health, 2011.

40. Ibid.

41. Hancock, Peter A., HC Neil Ganey, and James L. Szalma. "Performance under stress: A re-evaluation of a foundational low of psychology." In 23rd Annual Army Science Conference. 2002.

42. Harvard Health, 2011.

43. Ibid.

44. Ibid.

45. Ibid.

46. Hannibal, 2014.

47. Ibid.

48. Ibid.

49. Ibid.

50. Akil, 2019.

51. McEwen, Bruce S., Jason D. Gray, and Carla Nasca. "Recognizing resilience: Learning from the effects of stress on the brain." Neurobiology of stress 1 (2015): 1-11.

52. Ibid.

53. Raio, Candace M., and Elizabeth A. Phelps. "The influence of acute stress on the regulation of conditioned fear." Neurobiology of stress 1 (2015): 134-146.

54. McEwen, 2015.

55. Bergland, Christopher. "Chronic Stress Can Damage Brain Structure and Connectivity." Psychology Today, 2014. Retrieved from https://www.psychologytoday.com/us/blog/the-athletes-way/201402/chronic-stress-can-damage-brain-structure-and-connectivity

56. McEwen, Bruce S. "Brain on stress: How the social environment gets under the skin." PNAS, 2012. Retrieved from https://www.pnas.org/content/109/Supplement_2/17180.full

57. Goodreads. "Quotable quote." Website, 2020. Retrieved from https://www.goodreads.com/quotes/95080-educating-the-mind-without-educating-the-heart-is-no-education

58. Oleksowicz, Michał. "Aristotle on the heart and brain." European Journal of Science and Theology 14, no. 3 (2018): 77-94.

59. Amour, J. A. "Neurocardiology-anatomical and functional principles." Boulder Creek, California: Institute of HeartMath (2003).

60. HeartMath Institute. "Mysteries of the heart." Website, 2016. Retrieved from https://www.heartmath.org/resources/infographic/mysteries-of-the-heart/

61. HeartMath Institute. "The science of HeartMath." Website, n.d. Retrieved from https://www.heartmath.com/science/

62. Ogawa, Tsuneo, and Adolfo J. de Bold. "The heart as an endocrine organ." Endocrine connections 3, no. 2 (2014): R31-R44.

63. Gutkowska, J., M. Jankowski, S. Mukaddam-Daher, and S. M. McCann. "Oxytocin is a cardiovascular hormone." Brazilian Journal of Medical and Biological Research 33, no. 6 (2000): 625-633.

64. Goodreads. "Quotable quote." Website, 2020. Retrieved from https://www.goodreads.com/quotes/44630-when-the-heart-speaks-the-mind-finds-it-indecent-to

65. HeartMath Institute. "The science of HeartMath." Website, n.d. Retrieved from https://www.heartmath.com/science/

66. HeartMath Institute. "Heart brain communication." Website, n.d. Retrieved from https://www.heartmath.org/research/science-of-the-heart/heart-brain-communication/

67. Ibid.

68. Ibid.

69. Gutkowska, 2000.

70. HeartMath Institute. "Heart brain communication." Website, n.d. Retrieved from https://www.heartmath.org/research/science-of-the-heart/heart-brain-communication/

71. Ibid.

72. Secretario, Mag. "What's the Meaning of Sleep & Emotions?" GoodLifeSleep.com, 2019. Retrieved from https://goodlifesleep.com/whats-the-meaning-of-sleep-emotions/

73. Billman, George E. "Heart rate variability–a historical perspective." Frontiers in physiology 2 (2011): 86.

74. Ibid.

75. HeartMath Institute. "The science of HeartMath." Website, n.d. Retrieved from https://www.heartmath.com/science/

76. Ibid.

77. Ibid.

78. Ibid.

79. Ibid.

80. Ibid.

81. Ibid.

82. HeartMath Institute. "About us." Website, n.d. Retrieved from https://www.heartmath.org/about-us/

83. HeartMath Institute. "The science of HeartMath." Website, n.d. Retrieved from https://www.heartmath.com/science/

84. Ibid.

85. Ibid.

86. Gershon, Michael. The second brain: a groundbreaking new understanding of nervous disorders of the stomach and intestine. HarperCollins, 2019.

87. University of Gothenburg. "Surface area of the digestive tract much smaller than previously thought." ScienceDaily. www.sciencedaily.com/releases/2014/04/140423111505.htm

88. University of California - Los Angeles. "Study shows how serotonin and a popular anti-depressant affect the gut's microbiota." ScienceDaily. www.sciencedaily.com/releases/2019/09/190906092809.htm

89. Mayer, Emeran. The mind-gut connection: how the hidden conversation within our bodies impacts our mood, our choices, and our overall health. HarperCollins, 2018.

90. Damasio, Antonio R. "The somatic marker hypothesis and the possible functions of the prefrontal cortex." Philosophical Transactions of the Royal Society of London. Series B: Biological Sciences 351, no. 1346 (1996): 1413-1420.

91. Medical News Today. "New way for gut neurons to communicate with the brain." Website, 2020. Retrieved from https://www.medicalnewstoday.com/articles/new-way-for-gut-neurons-to-communicate-with-the-brain

92. Enders, Giulia."The surprisingly charming science of your gut." TED Talks, 2017. Retrieved from https://www.ted.com/talks/giulia_enders_the_sur- prisingly_charming_science_of_your_gut?language=en#t-2288

93. Carpenter, Siri, MD. "That gut feeling." APA.org. Retrieved from https://www. apa.org/monitor/2012/09/gut-feeling

94. Pennisi, Elizabeth. "Digging Deep into the Microbiome." (2011): 1008-1009.

95. Ibid.

96. Habib, Navaz. Activate Your Vagus Nerve: Unleash Your Body's Natural Ability to Heal. Simon and Schuster, 2019.

97. Ibid.

98. Ibid.

99. Habib, Navaz. Activate Your Vagus Nerve: Unleash Your Body's Natural Ability to Heal. Simon and Schuster, 2019.

100. Kok, Bethany E., Kimberly A. Coffey, Michael A. Cohn, Lahnna I. Catalino, Tan- ya Vacharkulksemsuk, Sara B. Algoe, Mary Brantley, and Barbara L. Fredrick- son. "How positive emotions build physical health: Perceived positive social connections account for the upward spiral between positive emotions and vagal tone." Psychological science 24, no. 7 (2013): 1123-1132.

101. Rosenberg, Stanley. Accessing the healing power of the vagus nerve: Self- help exercises for anxiety, depression, trauma, and autism. North Atlantic Books, 2017.

102. Ibid.

103. Enders, Giulia. Gut: The Inside Story of Our Body's Most Underrated Organ (Revised Edition). Greystone Books Ltd, 2018.

104. Mayer, 2018.

105. Rosenberg, 2017.